CHILD CUSTODY

A COMPLETE GUIDE FOR PARENTS

ENDORSEMENTS

"This is a great, practical, easy-to-read guide for all parents working through child custody issues. Empower yourself before you come to court by this read."
—*Kathleen McCarthy, Judge, Wayne County Circuit Court-Family Division*

"Dr. Jack Haynes and attorney Henry Gornbein have taken on the complex topic of child custody. They offer insightful analysis and practical strategies for those faced with custody and parenting time issues. Having both a legal and psychological approach to custody and parenting time issues results in the best outcomes for both parents and children."
—*Linda Hallmark, Judge, Oakland County Probate Court*

"Well-written and very informative. Recommended reading for anyone with parenting time/custody issues."
—*Mark Switalski, Judge, Macomb County Circuit Court-Family Division*

"This is an excellent book for helping parents navigate the family court system. It is easy to read, covers all relevant areas, and provides practical advice. A valuable resource and a must-read!"
—*James Bow, Ph.D., ABPP-Forensic Psychologist*

"This is a must-read for parents who are looking to increase their confidence in handling stressful custody circumstances. It is clear, useful, interesting, and easy to understand. Gornbein and Haynes have done a great job in helping parents facing a child custody dispute."
—*Steve Peck, Divorce Source Radio, Founder and Host*

"I don't think I have read a more thorough and thoughtful book on the topic. The information is current, the research and advice is sound, and the mission is clear: to assist everyone involved in a child custody dispute focus their attention on doing what is best for the children. It should be required reading for all lawyers and mental health professionals considering working in this area. And for parents, it is an invaluable resource for demystifying a terrifying process."
—*Daniel Bloom, Esq., Attorney, Former Family Court Judge,*
  Mediator, Arbitrator, and Guardian Ad Litem

"Gornbein and Haynes provide a much-needed and simple guide for parents going through divorce. They address the legal process and the psychological issues that may be present and considered by the courts and custody evaluators, answering questions parents may have about this very stressful time in their family. This book, written by a lawyer and a psychologist, is like having a built-in adviser assisting parents as they proceed with divorce."
—*Robin M. Deutsch, Ph.D., ABPP-Professor of Clinical Psychology,*
  William James College

"A child custody dispute is one of the most difficult and stressful experiences a parent has to face. Navigating such an experience without a clear understanding of what to expect and what is realistic can have a devastating effect on a child's development. Dr. Jack Haynes and Henry Gornbein provide a helpful tool to assist parents in navigating this difficult experience, understanding and reinforcing the absolute need to place the child's well-being above all else."
—*David S. Mendelson, Esq., Attorney, Past President of Michigan*
  Chapter of the American Academy of Matrimonial Lawyers

"This book distills the collective wisdom of two of the most experienced child custody professionals in our field. It explains the legal processes and relevant psychological concepts in a way that parents who may become involved in the family justice system can understand and apply to their situation. The authors systematically and comprehensively demystify the often overwhelming complexity of the separation and divorce transition when disputes arise between co-parents about the best interests of their children."
—*Matthew J. Sullivan, Ph.D., Forensic Psychology-President, Association of Family*
  and Conciliation Courts, Co-Founder of Overcoming Barriers Inc.

"This book should be required reading for every parent. It addresses current, relevant legal issues and provides guidance regarding challenging psychological concerns."
—*Susan E. Cohen, Esq., Attorney, Past President of Michigan Chapter*
  of the American Academy of Matrimonial Lawyers

"*Child Custody* is an amazingly complete primer, based on experience, and full of wisdom."
—*Daniel A. Schnaar, M.D., Practicing Pediatrician and Assistant Professor,*
  William Beaumont/Oakland University School of Medicine

CHILD CUSTODY

A COMPLETE GUIDE FOR PARENTS

HENRY S. GORNBEIN, ESQ., AND JACK P. HAYNES, PH.D.

MOMENTUM BOOKS

MOMENTUM BOOKS L.L.C.
TROY, MI

Printed and bound in the U.S.A.
Published by Momentum Books, L.L.C., a subsidiary of Hour Media, L.L.C.
5750 New King Drive, Suite 100
Troy, Michigan 48098
www.momentumbooks.com

ISBN-13: 978-1-938018-22-0
Library of Congress Control Number: 2020911421

Dedication

Our book is dedicated to our lovely wives,
Debra Gornbein and Suzanne Haynes,
in appreciation of their patience
and understanding.

Henry S. Gornbein, Esq.
Jack P. Haynes, Ph.D.

CONTENTS

INTRODUCTION

Raising children is one of life's most important missions. When it comes to custody issues, parents too often find themselves caught up in a confusing and frightening legal system. This makes that mission all the more difficult.

We, the authors of *Child Custody: A Complete Guide for Parents* — psychologist Jack P. Haynes, Ph.D., and attorney Henry S. Gornbein, Esq. — have more than 90 years of combined experience working with child custody from two different perspectives. This book presents both points of view — legal and psychological — which are essential for parents to consider regarding custody and parenting time.

We present chapters from our perspectives and address factors that affect children from infancy to adulthood. We share our expertise to help parents understand the legal system when it comes to their children.

Our ultimate goal is to help parents stay out of court while providing information and ideas about what is best for children — legally and psychologically.

Chapter themes include legal custody, physical custody, parenting time, psychological evaluations, and all of the other issues parents could face as they navigate the legal system. The authors address couples going through a divorce as well as those who never married, same-sex issues, the impact of the internet, social media, religion, ethnicity, and cultural backgrounds.

We cover trials and alternative ways to resolve your cases out of court, along with tips involving ways to move on with life while being the best-possible parents once the legal battle is over.

Our hope is that upon reading *Child Custody*, separating or divorcing parents will be better able to handle the myriad issues involving their children — eventualities that may or may not happen, depending upon your situation. Knowledge is power.

The goal here is to demystify the legal system. We present sound, practical advice from both legal and psychological perspectives. We lay out a path for parents grappling with issues involving custody, parenting time, and parenting choices regarding their children from infancy through adolescence.

This book provides answers to questions regarding child custody — even those that parents may not have thought to ask. In a rapidly changing world, we hope that readers of this book will walk away better informed and more capable of achieving their mission of doing what is best for their children.

—Henry S. Gornbein, Esq., and Jack P. Haynes, Ph.D.
June, 2020

CHAPTER

1

THEN AND NOW

I n ancient times — and even today in some parts of the world — there existed the principle that a father had an absolute property right to his children. In some countries today, a mother is to raise children to a certain age, and then the father becomes the primary parent in the event of a divorce when they are older.

In Michigan, where we practice, and also throughout the United States during the 1950s and 1960s, there was a strong presumption that a mother was always the better parent. We also had a tender years presumption that the mother of a young child was almost always the parent to receive custody.

Early in our careers, child custody was governed by the reality that Mom would receive custody and Dad would see the children on alternate weekends from Friday until Sunday and perhaps one evening per week for dinner. Joint custody, or primary custody to Dad, was infrequent and almost unheard of.

EQUAL OPPORTUNITY PARENTING

Then things changed. In Michigan, the Child Custody Act of 1970 defined 12 Best Interests of the Child Factors and required their consideration regarding what was in the best interests of the children when deciding custody. Many other states began to adopt similar best interests statutes as well. Was change immediate? Absolutely not. Change has been gradual.

In Michigan in the 1970s, even with the Best Interests Factors, the general rule was still that Mom was favored for custody. In most cases, especially with young children, Dad would have some visitation and kids spent the majority of the time with Mom. About 20 years ago, "visitation" was changed to "parenting time" in Michigan because each parent is parenting with a child or children, rather than just visiting. "Parenting time" is a much more realistic term, reflecting the change in parenting responsibilities.

What did it take to have a father awarded primary custody? A lot. Conditions had to shock the conscience of the judge, which was not easy.

We have seen a lot of changes since then. When we started practicing, there were very few female judges or attorneys. In our geographical area, a majority of the judges in family law are women who work and who also are parents. Also, many women practice law on a full-time basis while they are parents.

Due to economic necessity in many households today, both parents work outside the home. The stay-at-home mom is not as common. In some cases, Dad has become "Mr. Mom," with the mother being the primary breadwinner.

There has also been a shift in attitudes. The presumptions favoring a mother, even with young children, are changing based upon economic realities and the fact that more and more judges and attorneys believe that both men and women can be good, if not excellent, parents.

More and more fathers are obtaining primary physical custody and the norm is evolving to various types of shared physical custody. Fathers are expected to have more responsibility based on the view that children need both parents.

The concept of the weekend dad is becoming less frequent. Part of this is due to the attitudes of experts who are strongly recommending shared custodial arrangements. Also, these arrangements often work better.

SHARED CUSTODY ARRANGEMENTS

The authors have observed many shared custodial plans where the children have what is called a 2-2-5 arrangement. For example, this means that the children will spend Monday and Tuesday overnight with one parent and Wednesday and Thursday overnight with the other parent. The parties then alternate weekends from Friday through Monday morning so that the children never go more than five days without seeing the other parent — hence the 2-2-5 formula.

In many cases, there is some form of shared custody, but time apportionment is not necessarily 50-50. It can be 60-40 or 2/3-1/3. In some situations, it has become a numbers game because child support is tied to the number of overnights the children spend with each parent and the incomes of each parent. It should not be this way.

Where are we now? We recently have been involved in cases with infants where the courts have ordered shared 50-50 custody. We had one situation where breastfeeding was an issue — one of us tried the case and the other was the expert. The court decided on an arrangement that at age 2, the child would spend six out of 14 overnights with the father.

We now have a movement in which some people believe that there should be a strong presumption favoring shared equal custody in every case with children. This will in essence throw out the 12 Best Interests Factors of the Child Custody Act and require a parent who is opposed to an equal custodial arrangement to show by clear and convincing evidence that there should not be equal custody.

We believe that as lawyers, psychotherapists, evaluators, and judges, we must still look at our clients and their situations regarding custody on a case-by-case basis. Are we trending too much to a cookie-cutter approach? Are we becoming guilty of trying to treat every divorce and family the same? The best interests of the children as dictated by the 12 Factors that define them by statute and case law is a system that works. This is true in Michigan and other states, where the key is what is in the best interests of the children and not necessarily what Mom or Dad want. It requires lawyers, judges, mental health professionals, referees, and family counselors to look at each case and determine what is in the best interests of the children. This approach often produces the best results for children.

Does a shared custodial arrangement along with joint legal custody make sense in most cases? Yes, but there are many cases where some variation is necessary, and in some divorces or breakups of unmarried couples, shared physical custody is a disaster. In some situations, one parent has been the primary parent and caretaker and the best interests dictate that the parent continue to be so. Anyone dealing with a custody situation must reflect on what is best for the children and not just on what a parent wants.

We have come a long way regarding the custody of our children. The saying that it takes a village to raise a child conveys a lot of truth. Today, grandparents, aunts, and uncles may all participate. There is also more conflict where people cannot agree or cannot get along with former in-laws, parents, or grandparents. Custody is continually in a state of flux. Above all else, it is important to look at what is best for your child.

TAKEAWAYS

We have gone from an era where there was a presumption that "mother knows best" to one where some type of shared custody is the norm. It is important to discuss your situation with your attorney and carefully consider the best interests of your child.

Notes

_____

_____

_____

_____

_____

_____

_____

_____

_____

_____

_____

_____

_____

_____

_____

_____

_____

_____

_____

_____

_____

_____

_____

_____

_____

CHAPTER 2

THE BEST INTERESTS FACTORS

Most states have their own version of a Best Interests statute, and Michigan is no different. In every custody case or visitation/parenting time dispute in Michigan, the courts must follow the Best Interests statute, as detailed here. The law is the same for unmarried as well as married parents.

1. The love, affection, and other emotional ties existing between the parties involved and the child;
2. The capacity and disposition of the parties involved to give the child love, affection, and guidance and continuation of the educating and raising of the children in their religion or creed, if any;
3. The capacity and disposition of the parties involved to provide the child with food, clothing, medical care, or other remedial care recognized and permitted under the laws of the state in place of medical care, and other material needs;
4. The length of time the child has lived in a stable, satisfactory environment, and the desirability of maintaining continuity;
5. The permanence, as a family unit, of the existing or proposed custodial home or homes;
6. The moral fitness of the parties involved;
7. The mental and physical health of the parties involved;
8. The home, school, and community record of the child;
9. The reasonable preference of the child, if the court deems the child to be of sufficient age to express preference;
10. The willingness and ability of each of the parents to facilitate and encourage close and continuing parent-child relationships between the child and the other parent;
11. Domestic violence, regardless of whether the violence was directed against or witnessed by the child;
12. Any other factor considered by the court to be relevant to the particular child custody dispute.

MAKING A PLAN

Issues involving child custody must be fact-based. Each case is different. It is important to remember that we often get hung up on labels. More and more in our practices where custody is an issue, we try to frame the case without using the words "physical custody." The key is to come up with a solution where each parent has a specific parenting plan with a designated number of overnights with the children of the relationship.

There is no requirement in Michigan to use the terms "joint physical custody" or "primary physical custody." There is a requirement that legal custody be stated as sole or joint, but that is different.

Most experts in the area of child custody oppose a mandatory presumption favoring 50-50 joint custody. The specific parenting arrangement typically works best depending on the facts of the circumstances.

For example, here's the way that 2-2-5 model discussed in Chapter 1 might play out: The mother has every Monday and Tuesday, the father every Wednesday and Thursday, and the parents alternate weekends from Friday through Monday morning. One parent transports the child at the beginning of each transfer and the other parent returns the child.

Another possible time apportionment scenario can be alternating parenting time weeks with Wednesday overnight time spent with the mom or dad who does not have parenting time on the upcoming weekend.

What counts most is encouraging a cooperative spirit between parents. There can be, for example, a shared custodial arrangement where one parent has eight out of 14 overnights. A typical child will not know the difference between seven, eight, or nine overnights in a two-week period.

Another possible parenting time arrangement, if it fits the parenting experiences of the parties, is alternate weekends from Friday until Monday and then two overnights during the week in Week One and an overnight in Week Two. There can be five out of 14, with one parent having alternate weekends and one overnight each week.

ONE SIZE DOES NOT FIT ALL

The possibilities are many, and the arrangement should be based on the nature and history of the parent-child relationships. Too much back and forth is undesirable.

Some arrangements that we have seen appear to foster equal time, but in fact are disruptive to the children, who have to adjust to living in two different residences with different house rules and patterns. Sometimes it is proposed that parents alternate co-parenting time daily. This would mean the child alternates parental residences daily, alternating weekends. This could be referred to as the King Solomon Solution, but in fact it sacrifices the interests of the child to satisfy a parent's need for a feeling of fairness. The child or children experience far too much back and forth, which is clearly not in the best interests of the child.

For the purpose of arranging equal time, it can be useful to consider a longer perspective, such as the full year. To that purpose, one parent could have more co-parenting time during the school year and the second parent could have additional time during the holidays and summer.

The problem is that a lot of parents are intent on counting overnights and lose sight of what is best for their children. Instead of counting days, they would do better to focus on their child's likely comfort level.

OTHER SPECIFIC OPTIONS

It is also important to spell out holiday arrangements. As an example, a holiday and vacation schedule can be built around alternating the major holidays of Memorial Day, the Fourth of July, Labor Day, Halloween, Thanksgiving, Christmas Eve, and Christmas Day. Sometimes New Year's Eve/Day are included in the schedule.

Other holidays can be included based on religious beliefs. These can include Easter, Jewish holidays, Islamic Holy Days such as Eid and Ramadan, Hindu celebrations, African-American holidays, Greek Orthodox holidays, and others. It depends on the family.

A good schedule typically alternates the child or children's birthdays and has Father's Day with Dad and Mother's Day with Mom. In addition, the schedule might include each parent's birthday.

Some people will have the holidays as the entire time period — for example, Memorial Day and Labor Day weekends. Thanksgiving can become an extended weekend as well.

Christmas vacation can be apportioned in ways that fit the specific traditions of the parties. Some settlement agreements provide for one parent having parenting time from the day after school gets out until noon on Christmas Day, with the other parent having parenting time from that point until New Year's Day. This can alternate and will differ somewhat each year with the variability of school vacation times.

Parents often alternate February/Winter Break as well as the Spring/Easter Break. During the summer, the normal schedule can continue with each parent having a week or two for vacation time or, in some instances, the parents rotating every other week.

It's important to remember that one size does not fit all. Every case is different, and what makes sense for one family might not make sense for others. A lot depends upon how well the parents communicate as well as the job and vacation schedules of each parent.

And parents should be flexible during negotiations. The more rigid and inflexible the communication is between the parents, the more important it is to spell out every detail. In some relationships, identifying to-the-minute pick-up and drop-off times and specific locations for those exchanges can become critical.

Sadly, we have seen too many cases where children have to be exchanged at a local police station. Though sometimes necessary, that sends a negative message to the children involved.

COMMUNICATION IS CRITICAL

Another important issue is communication. Some parents communicate poorly or minimally. In many cases, as part of a settlement agreement and final order, there will be a clause that the child or children shall speak on a daily basis to the absent parent without interference. In cases where the parents are in different states, Skype or another form of visual communication is often useful.

People are also communicating more by text and email. Where there is a lot of nastiness or a failure to communicate properly, services such as Our Family Wizard (OFW), a password protected online tool, provide a vehicle for communication for a small annual fee. On the OFW system, all communications are written and recorded. OFW encourages parents to be more civil by using that process.

Another important issue is that orders regarding custody and parenting time are always modifiable until the child or children reach the age of 18. An arrangement that makes sense for an infant or toddler often doesn't translate for a child of 8 or 9. We have been involved in issues over infants and have had courts call for shared parenting time arrangements that take breastfeeding patterns into account, for example.

Teenagers differ from young children. Teenagers often want to spend as little time as possible with their parents and want to be with their friends, or are very involved in school and extracurricular activities.

Take the typical dialogue with a teenager about his or her day:

Parent: "Where did you go?"

Teen: "Out."

Parent: "What did you do?"

Teen: "Nothing."

We often tell our clients that, not surprisingly, teenage custody battles are as follows: "You take them!" "No, you can have them."

As the saying goes, "Little children, little problems, and big children, big problems." There is a lot of truth to that. Teenagers can be challenging.

And children of all ages can be manipulative. Even in the best of circumstances, they can try to play one parent off another. But with separated or divorced parents, it's so much easier for children to get under their parents' skin in this way. Maybe they will say that "Dad lets me do this" or "Mom lets me do that." The reality is that parents will always be manipulated. That's why being able to communicate is critical to making sure that parents who don't live together aren't being manipulated more than necessary.

TAKEAWAYS

Custody is complicated and ever-changing. It is critical to remember that this chapter's purpose is to provide you with some understanding of the best interests of your children and how that affects custody and parenting time. We urge parents to talk to an attorney and/or psychotherapist before making any decisions regarding disputes in this area. Proceeding on your own can be fraught with peril.

Notes

_____

_____

_____

_____

_____

_____

_____

_____

_____

_____

_____

_____

_____

_____

_____

_____

_____

_____

_____

_____

_____

_____

_____

_____

_____

_____

_____

_____

CHAPTER 3

JOINT LEGAL CUSTODY — AND DECISIONS

M

ichigan has statutory and case law dealing with legal custody and with where the children will reside. In this chapter, we explore the meaning and impact of legal custody.

In final court orders or judgments regarding a divorce with child custody, it is helpful if the language used defines specifically what is meant by legal custody. In most cases, the parties to a divorce or custody dispute share joint legal custody as well as some form of a shared or joint physical custody arrangement. Legal custody is an issue that comes up often in psychological evaluations as well as in working with people regarding parenting time and custodial issues.

When joint legal custody is being considered, courts often weigh the capacity of each party to fulfill the following requirements:

- Each parent shall foster, encourage, and support the relationship between the children and the other parent.

- Each parent shall consult and attempt to agree before major decisions are made affecting the child's/children's education, enrichment activities, camp, travel, and medical problems — or if they cannot agree, seek an Order of the Court.
- Each parent shall have equal access to medical and educational records of the minor child(ren).
- Each parent shall notify the other of any emergencies relating to the minor child(ren) and notify and give the other parent an opportunity to be present for all routine medical, dental, optical, and psychological treatment.
- Each parent shall keep the other parent informed of the whereabouts of the child(ren) and his/her/their own whereabouts in the event of a medical or other emergency.

- The parties shall inform and be informed about school, music or sports, and other enrichment activities of the child(ren), and be provided an opportunity for parenting.
- While each party has the physical custody of the minor child(ren) that party shall be responsible for all routine decisions regarding the minor child(ren).
- The parent exercising parenting time shall drive the children to and from such activities.
- Each parent shall be permitted to have daily telephone contact or video Skype at a reasonable time and of a reasonable duration when the children are with the other parent. Each parent shall allow and encourage the daily telephone contact.
- Each party shall provide the other party with his or her present address, phone number, and subsequent changes.
- Neither party shall disparage the other parent in the presence of the minor children, and each party recognizes that they both wish to encourage and foster a close relationship between both parties and the children. Further, neither party shall disparage the other to third parties in the presence of the minor children or allow third parties to disparage the other parent in the minor children's presence.
- Each party, if they maintain firearms in their homes, shall keep all firearms and ammunition locked in a gun case at all times during his or her parenting time.
- Each parent shall keep the children out of any disputes that they as parents are involved in with the goal that the children shall be kept out of any legal battles regarding a divorce or any other issues that should stay between the parents.

LET KIDS BE KIDS

Parents should not involve their children in legal disputes and should put their children's best interests ahead of their own grievances against the other parent. Sadly, both of us have been involved in many disputes involving interpretations of joint legal custody over the years.

We have been involved in extreme cases where judges have ruled that because the parents apparently cannot communicate and do not put their children's best interests first, there is to be sole legal custody with one parent having authority to decide on issues such as medical treatment, school-related issues, and other decisions that should normally be made jointly.

Many disputes occur over school-related issues. This can involve whether a child should attend public, parochial, or private school. We also have dealt with cases involving home schooling versus public schooling.

Geographic location can be disputed. Often when a couple splits up or there is a divorce, one or the other will move out of the school district. If the parents cannot agree on the location, then the court needs to step in.

As an example, a mother moved due to an excellent job opportunity an hour away. The child then came to be placed in a school one hour away, where neither parent resides. The result is that a 6-year-old who previously spent every other day with Mom and Dad is forced to spend an hour each way to and from school when Mom is driving and over a half hour each way to and from school when Dad is driving. These are some of the issues that courts have to deal with in the area of joint legal custody.

Special needs of a child also can be a source of dispute and may necessitate court intervention. Disputes can relate to what are appropriate services for the child and if there is a need for special education or tutors. Should a child be kept back a year for kindergarten if he or she is not emotionally ready?

Both of us have had cases involving nutritional issues, such as breastfeeding and the appropriate time for a child to be weaned. Controversies over food allergies and the appropriate treatment have been raised in many cases, since parents may disagree.

Involvement in extracurricular activities can be a source of conflict for separated parents. Should a child play soccer, baseball, or hockey? Take dance or figure skate? Go to day camp or overnight camp? How can parents who disagree decide? Can they cooperate and reach mutual decisions? Sometimes the issue is not only whether a child shall participate, but often, who is going to pay for it. In one situation, the cost for a child in figure skating approached $30,000 per year.

Religion is another area of controversy. This is especially true where parents are of different faiths or have different belief systems. People even fight over baptisms, confirmations, bar and bat mitzvahs, and regular attendance in Sunday School.

Medical decisions are included under joint legal custody. There has been much litigation recently regarding whether a child should be vaccinated. Most courts have ruled that a child should be vaccinated.

Other issues have related to whether a child should be in psychotherapy. Or what about elective surgery? Braces? Sometimes parents battle over whether their child should be on a stimulant medication like Ritalin, Concerta, or Adderall, or should take no medication at all.

Children's haircut style, hair length, and attire can be disputed. The style of clothing and who pays for it can be argued.

Cell phone possession and use as well as playing video games can be disputed. Amount of usage and degree of monitoring can be sources of disagreement. What about computers or other electronic devices? Who is monitoring them? Who is protecting the child from predators?

Also, computer games can be an issue. Severe addiction to computer games has resulted in situations where children have dropped out of school for inpatient treatment.

Parents must watch and monitor children's access to electronic devices.

Children can be much more sophisticated than their parents when it comes to this technology in our high-tech world.

Travel, vacation location, and passports can be sources of contention. For example, which parent keeps the child's passport? At what age should a child travel alone? If a parent is from another country, this can become a major issue.

LOOK FOR SOLUTIONS

While it is easy to squabble, that is not usually helpful to your children. Remember that the more you fight, the more you are likely to be hurting your child or children. Step back and think about what is best for your child and not what you want. Do not use your child as a weapon against the other parent, because all you are doing is causing more pain for your child. You also are showing your child that his/her parents are not able to work things out in their best interests.

The bottom line: When it comes to interpreting joint legal custody language and what is in the best interests of your child or children, it is important to look for solutions. Try your very best to settle disputes with your soon-to-be ex-partner. When you end up in court and a judge must make the decision, usually no one ends up happy. You lose control if you cannot find a way to resolve matters between yourselves.

It can be helpful to consult an attorney or mental health professional to find solutions to these problems and avoid the need for court intervention. Sadly, it's not uncommon that people come to an attorney or psychotherapist after the damage has been done and after a wrong decision has been made. Try to be proactive on these issues — not reactive.

PARENTING TIME IN A PANDEMIC

In the interest of being proactive, we also wanted to address the coronavirus pandemic that began as this book went to press.

The most important issues with children always include safety and mental health. Reliable sources of information include the Centers for Disease Control (CDC), UNICEF, and the American Psychological Association (APA) websites. At the time of publication, these websites were:

www.cdc.gov/coronavirus/2019-ncov/daily-life-coping/children.html
www.unicef.org/coronavirus/keep-your-child-safe-online-at-home-covid-19
www.apa.org/topics/covid-19

When it comes to physical safety, the CDC, for example, recommends practicing social distancing and frequent hand-washing, especially if your child has been in a public place. Check with the CDC site for other physical health and safety recommendations. Watch your child for signs of illness. Also observe if your child is displaying excess sadness or anxiety or has disrupted sleeping or eating patterns.

Your child may be using the internet more. Among other things the sites recommend is having a direct dialogue with your children about how and with whom they communicate online. If you have not done so before, establish clear rules for use of devices. Be sure the programs have antivirus software, and that the privacy settings are on. This is particularly important for young children.

Make sure your child understands issues involving strangers online. Also help your children avoid misinformation and age-inappropriate content. Emphasize positive interactions for them with their friends and relatives. If appropriate, consider establishing a regular audio/video contact pattern for your child with the other parent, especially if your child is in a stay-at-home or quarantine format.

Do not use this circumstance as an opportunity to limit contact with the other parent. Always act in harmony with fostering healthy contact and maintaining emotional attachment between your child and the other parent.

If your child is doing online schooling, be familiar with school policies and requirements. Journal writing can be constructive. Use helplines to report cyberbullying and inappropriate content.

Encourage your child to be active indoors and out — no hour after hour of television or video games. Activity is important for physical as well as mental health. Often a flexible general plan for the day can be helpful with children. Fun, learning, handling some responsibilities depending on your child's age, and social interactions all are important. Adjust activities to the age and developmental level of your child.

The American Psychological Association addresses a wide variety of topics related to COVID-19 at its website in the section "COVID-19 Information and Resources." It is continually updated.

Such a unique and challenging time in history can be an opportunity for families to get to know each other better. It also is a time for individuals, including children, to learn about themselves more.

As a parent, this is a time to emphasize resilience, problem-solving, patience, and flexibility. This is an opportunity to model empathy and kindness. It's a time of meeting new challenges.

TAKEAWAYS

Joint legal custody is extremely important. It affects religious, medical, and school-related decisions. It is important to understand the ramifications of your actions as you move forward and raise your child or children after you and your spouse or significant other have agreed to go your separate ways.

Notes

_____

_____

_____

_____

_____

_____

_____

_____

_____

_____

_____

_____

_____

_____

_____

_____

_____

_____

_____

_____

_____

_____

_____

_____

_____

_____

CHAPTER

PSYCHOLOGICAL ISSUES: IT'S COMPLICATED

Divorce and/or permanent separations are unavoidably disruptive to everyone in the family unit. Living circumstances and financial arrangements are altered. Often, supportive relationships with family and friends shift.

For children, the end of cohabiting parental relationships may mean reduced parental income to support them and disrupted peer and family relationships due to changes in residence and school locations. It is not uncommon for children to lose focus on academics or sports if their home circumstances have changed substantially. Even when changes are positive, they can impose stress on children because change requires adjustment. Simply put, it's stressful for everyone.

Spousal abuse can be part of the motivation to divorce. This can affect the nature of the post-relationship of the adults as well as the parent-child relationship. Abuse is a negative complication to a positive post-relationship, for both the adults and children. Negative outcomes also are more likely when significant mental illness and substance abuse are present. Courts often use the help of professionals to assess the effects of abuse, mental illness, and/or substance abuse on children.

It is important to try to insulate children from stressors during the divorce process as well as during the post-relationship. Children should not be informed or knowledgeable about spousal conflicts and shortcomings, the legal process or strategies, settlement issues, and even court dates. These issues are beyond the ability of a child to process and can divert attention from normal child development. Exposing children to such stressors may — depending on their age — cause them to regress, display isolative behavior and sadness, become more irritable and disruptive, or exhibit symptoms of tiredness or sleep difficulties.

Typical custody determinations are final. Families move forward with their changed circumstances, using court orders as their guidelines. There is usually no need for continued court involvement. However, sometimes circumstances change and modifications are necessary. This may require a return to court involvement. Sometimes modification of custody arrangements may be less arduous than the initial custody determination, though that may depend on how the living circumstances have changed.

Effects of adjustments on adults and on children in contested custody situations are predominantly psychological and social in nature, depending on the specific changes. Examples of potential conflict areas include with whom the child lives, how much the children see each parent, and what sorts of experiences the child has with each parent in the new circumstances. The post-relationship effects on children depend in great measure on the feelings and behavior of the adults.

Parents who continue to be embittered about the ended relationship are more likely to have a negative effect on their children.

In general, the longer and more intense the conflict as observed by the children, the higher the likelihood for continuing problems. Parents who can relate to each other reasonably and work together post-relationship are more likely to facilitate the positive adjustment of their children to new circumstances.

The nature of the relationship between children and parents before the breakup typically is also related to the quality of the post-relationship adjustment of parents and children. The continuity of a positive relationship is a significant predictor of good adjustment, even as the divorce process can be disruptive.

Another very important aspect of post-relationship child adjustment is the extent to which both parents are committed to the importance of the children and their developmental and emotional needs.

SEIZE THE DAY

It would seem that a major goal of post-relationship parent-child relationships requires sufficient parenting time. There is likely no magic in brief but intense post-relationship parent-child contact. To a certain extent, quality of time necessarily includes some quantity of time. Regularity of contact and predictability of contact also are important.

It is also helpful to have some involvement by both parents in routine and repeating events, despite separate living circumstances, if that is possible. Examples include parents jointly participating in school and other extracurricular events, medical care, meeting and being familiar with the friends of the children, extended family involvement by the children with both sides of the family, sharing some holiday or birthday meals, and agreement on waking and bedtime patterns and rituals. Involvement and consistency by both parents provides a healthy structure for the child. This requires maturity and some setting aside of differences by both parents.

Transitioning from one household to another involves some degree of stress for most children, given these changes are done on a timeline established by adults — not by the children themselves. It is not uncommon for a child to show signs of upset or reluctance to leave one household for another, to the point of protesting with sadness, anger, or tears.

It also is not uncommon for a child entering the other household to exhibit signs of withdrawal, isolation, and reluctance to reengage with the other parent. This pattern can be repeated at transition times, even when both parents are attempting to do their best. Such reactions from children do not mean the arrangement is bad. It's not necessarily an indication that things are not working out at one of the households. Children just need time to adjust.

Adjustment time is important whether the parent-child co-parenting time is frequent, or if it is less frequent because of a relocation by one parent. Parents do not always maintain exactly the same rules at both households, which is part of the stress for children and another reason why they need time to adjust. But it is important for there to be as much consistency of parental expectations as possible between the two households.

More research needs to take place to better understand the characteristics of positive parent-child relationships. In this regard, it is important for both parents to keep the focus on the best interests of their children.

By definition, time is passing and time is limited — the children are growing older and there is less parent-child time available because time is now split between the parents. As the saying goes, "Seize the day!" Enjoy your time with your child.

TAKEAWAYS

Divorce — or child custody disputes when a nonmarital arrangement ends — means myriad changes that are stressful for both parents and children. Parents can do a lot to help smooth the process for children, shielding them from the messy adult parts and making the unavoidable disruptions in households and daily routines as palatable as possible.

Notes

CHAPTER

CHOOSING AN ATTORNEY

Selecting the right attorney is critical before you embark on litigation regarding your children. It is important to have an experienced family law attorney represent you in issues regarding custody or parenting time.

Co-author Henry S. Gornbein has been practicing family law for more than 45 years, and has seen myriad changes regarding how custody and parenting time are handled by the courts. We are now in an era where many judges will at least entertain the idea of shared and often equal custodial arrangements with your children. Custody and parenting time matters often are complex and allow for a variety of approaches — some effective, some not.

You do not want an attorney who only dabbles in family law. You not only want someone who has handled many divorce cases with children, but also who can deal with issues that can be out of the routine. You do not want an attorney with a high-volume practice who takes the approach that one size fits all. You want to make sure that you are given the attention that is required to properly handle your child-related case. Select an attorney who solves problems, rather than one who creates them.

How do you find a good custody attorney? Check with friends and family. Often a good psychotherapist will make referrals. There are also rating services. An example is the American Academy of Matrimonial Lawyers, an organization of leading family law lawyers throughout the country with chapters in nearly every state and metropolitan area. Check out the Academy website at *AAML.org*. Other rating services include *SuperLawyers.com*, *AVVO.com*, *BestLawyers.com/America*, and *MartindaleHubbell.com*. There are other rating services, but these are among the most well-known.

Also, review a prospective lawyer's website. How long has he or she been practicing? To what organizations does the lawyer belong? Does he or she publish or blog?

OUT OF THE GATE: COMMUNICATE

When you meet with your attorney, it is imperative to be candid regarding your goals and wishes. A good attorney will give you a realistic appraisal of your options and what you can expect regarding your particular situation. Some lawyers may oversell a case and make unrealistic promises to scare you into retaining them. You do not want an attorney who will promise you the moon — but can't deliver.

Be careful. Ask many questions and remember that you not only want someone who is experienced and knowledgeable, but also with whom you can feel comfortable. They will represent you during a challenging time in your life and the life of your child.

Things to consider:

- An effective attorney for custody or parenting time should know the laws of your state regarding custody.
- There is a saying that a good attorney knows the law and a great attorney knows the judge. Don't hesitate to ask the attorney how familiar he or she is with the courts and judges in the area where your case will be handled.
- Don't hesitate to ask your attorney how many custody cases he or she has handled. Experience is crucial.
- Don't hesitate to ask about who will be handling your case. Will it be the attorney you meet with? Will it be handed over to another attorney? In some firms, one attorney does the intake and others do the actual work. Be familiar and comfortable with the attorney who actually handles your case. Some law firms use a team approach to family law matters. Make sure that you meet all of the members of your prospective legal team.
- Discuss communication options. Limited communication options can be problematic. Is your attorney available by phone, by email? How quickly will your calls be returned, your emails be responded to? Most clients would like to be called back within a couple of hours. It is important for an attorney to try to do that. The same holds true for emails. The custody of your children is very important, and good communication between you and your attorney is essential.
- If domestic violence is involved in your case, your attorney should be thoroughly familiar with those issues. He or she should be aware of the behaviors, patterns, and subtleties surrounding domestic violence. Domestic violence is broad and can involve physical as well as verbal and emotional abuse. Please see the chapter on this topic later in the book.

- A good custody attorney is not a child psychologist, but a family law attorney should be aware of the important psychological factors that accompany issues involving custody and parenting time of your children. In these situations, it is often important to have a skilled and experienced psychotherapist working with you and your children to help deal with and resolve many of the emotional conflicts and stressors that are often part of a child custody dispute.
- Your lawyer should be a good listener — and also empathic.

THE INITIAL CONSULTATION

The initial consultation sets the stage. This is the point where you consider a prospective attorney and the attorney is trying to get familiarized with your case and what the options may be.

Bring your questions to the initial consultation. It often helps to write them down in advance. Make sure that before you leave the meeting, all of your questions have been answered. Do not hesitate to ask anything. There are no dumb questions. Some suggestions for discussion include:

How do you view yourself as a parent? How do you view the other parent? Be prepared to discuss your children and your views regarding custody. What do you ideally want regarding custody and parenting time? What is most important? Where are you prepared to compromise?

In a marriage, you usually come to understand the other parent. In a situation where a short-term relationship produced a child, you may not know much about that person and how the other parent has been acting or will act and react with your child or children.

What is the best thing that you can say about the other parent? What are the worst things that you can say about the other parent?

What is the worst thing that he or she would say about you? What is the best thing that he or she would say about you as a parent? These are important discussion points.

Also consider your work schedule as well as the other parent's schedule, and the normal routine your child or children follow.

Most states have laws based upon the best interests of your child or children. Decisions are made not on what you think is in their best interests, but rather, on what a judge will view as their best interests based on the laws of your state. Be prepared to discuss the particular laws of the state you are in and how these laws may apply to your custody or parenting time dispute.

WHAT TO ASK

A good attorney will give you an honest appraisal based upon the facts that you present. Be candid and straightforward. Do not exaggerate, minimize, lie, or hold back. If you distort at the beginning of a relationship with an attorney, you will be complicating the situation and probably hurting yourself and your case.

Also inquire about how long the attorney has been practicing family law, how many custody cases the attorney has handled, and about fees and retainers. If the case is resolved early and the entire retainer is not used, is there a refund? If you retain a different attorney and change attorneys before the case is resolved, are you entitled to any portion of your retainer back? It is important to have at least an idea of what you will be charged.

In many cases, you can have a range of fees. Sadly, many cases take on a life of their own and it is often impossible to estimate the total cost. Most attorneys charge a retainer against an hourly rate. Some attorneys will charge a set or flat fee. The key is that you have an understanding as to how you will be charged before signing the retainer agreement. Discuss and review it before you sign it.

Ask the attorney if there is any reason why he or she may not be comfortable in representing you. If there are any issues regarding bias or comfort level, those should be discussed and resolved immediately. Trust your gut. If you feel comfortable with a prospective attorney, that is positive. If your gut reaction is negative, then examine the feeling and consider not retaining that particular attorney.

Ask the attorney about his or her attitude regarding mediation, negotiations, and ways to resolve a case without going to trial. Most cases are resolved short of trial, and you probably want to be represented by someone who is comfortable in negotiations and mediation, as these are key to resolving most custody matters.

Be certain that your attorney will provide you with copies of all pleadings, legal documents, correspondence, and any relevant information regarding your case. Your file should be identical to your attorney's file. It will help you be fully informed of every step in the process. This is critical, as you are dealing with your life and those of your children.

Ask for a timeline. Most cases must be completed in a year or less, though this will vary from state to state. It is important to ask your attorney about typical cases that are similar to yours and how long they usually take.

REASONABLE EXPECTATIONS

In a child custody or parenting time case, you are dealing with narrow issues based upon the best interests of your child or children — not the myriad other items that are part of a divorce, which involve a lot of trading and compromise.

Custody and parenting disputes can be more difficult because there are fewer questions to be resolved. You want to make sure that your attorney is working for you and not the other way around — that he or she is focused on the critical issues of your case. It is so important that you and your attorney work together as a team, focusing on any key child-related issues in your case. We can't emphasize it enough: Having the right attorney is critical. Select one who solves problems rather than one who creates them.

TAKEAWAYS

Before the initial consultation with an attorney, arm yourself with as much knowledge as possible about the practice and come with a list of questions so you can fully understand what to expect and what the possible outcomes may be regarding custody of your children or other child-related issues. Be sure the attorney is someone you like and have rapport with. Don't hesitate to ask about fees.

Notes

CHAPTER 6

ATTACHMENT: MAINTAINING EMOTIONAL BONDS

What is attachment? For our purposes, attachment in children involves the emotional bond between a parent and child, or between a nonparental caregiver and child. Attachment is characteristic not of the child or attachment figure, but of the relationship. A child who has been adopted can develop an equally significant emotional attachment with the adoptive parent(s).

Children can also form important attachments to secondary, nonparental figures like nannies, grandparents, and other relatives — even neighbors with a close relationship to a child.

Research indicates this is true not just in our culture, but cross-culturally. Also, research indicates attachment and its significance can extend throughout the lifespan.

Attachment has been studied from various psychological points of view, and much remains to be understood about this important concept. What we do know is based on various sources of information: observational studies, hard research, and clinical examples.

WHY ATTACHMENT IS IMPORTANT

The nature of attachment in child development has consequences for personality development and adjustment as well as how a person forms relationships later in life.

Consistency of attachment is important, tying in to the development of a person's sense of self and self-esteem. Children learn about the predictability of the world from the nature of their attachment. Disrupted or inconsistent attachment can impede the ability of a person to feel for and relate to others.

Attachment emerges around the age of six months and is most intense by the child's first or second birthday. Separation from attachment figures for children is difficult in those years. After about three years, though, the intensity decreases and most children can tolerate separation from their attachment figures. Older children who have difficulty with such separation are described as demonstrating separation anxiety.

Research has identified different styles of attachment, and it is thought that the styles are partly the result of interaction with the primary caregiver. The most important element in the development of attachment is the sensitivity of the caregiver to the needs of the child.

Most children experience secure attachment and feel confident the attachment figure will meet their needs. They seek the attachment figure when they are stressed and view the attachment figure as a safe reference point from which to explore the world. Securely attached infants are easily soothed. They seem to view the attachment figure as available, responsive, and helpful.

Some children are less secure and tend not to feel as confident that the attachment figure will meet their needs. They are more distant from the attachment figure both physically and emotionally. When under stress, they are less likely to seek contact with their attachment figure, perhaps because the attachment figure may withdraw or be unavailable physically or emotionally.

Some children can be described as forming insecure and ambivalent attachment. They may be clingy and dependent at times, while at others rejecting the attachment figure, sometimes unpredictably. These children typically feel less secure, are more difficult to soothe, and sometimes do not take comfort from the attachment figure. These behaviors typically emerge from inconsistent responses by the caregiver to the needs of the developing child.

Also, the nature of the attachment bond likely is passed on to the next generation. If a parent received mostly sensitive and well-balanced care as a child, they are likely to provide similar parenting. If a parent did not experience such nurturing, they can compensate for it, but it would require awareness and effort since it would have to be learned behavior.

Sometimes parents who themselves received unbalanced or insensitive care as children try to overcompensate and do the extreme opposite, which can result in other problems with the child. Parental self-awareness and focus on the experience of the child are most important.

DISRUPTED ATTACHMENT IN DIVORCE

Children typically lose significant periods of contact with one or more of their attachment figures when parents divorce. Also disruptive and detrimental to attachment, especially for young children, is the negative effect of parental yelling or violence. Sometimes in older children, poor school performance, home and school behavioral problems, and self-esteem disruption result when parents divorce. With adolescents, there can be delinquent behavior, sexual acting out, and clear academic shortcomings such as disengagement from school participation.

These negative consequences are not inevitable, with research showing mixed results of the effects of divorce on attachment. To some degree, the child's temperament may be either a protective factor or an exacerbating factor when it comes to divorce stressors. Gender and age also are characteristics that may have an impact on the effect of divorce stressors. Boys and girls sometimes react differently to reduced contact with their major attachment figure. Boys more frequently have a difficult time, especially seen in problematic academic performance and disruptive behavior. But these are generalizations — there are differences, depending on the particular child.

As for age, younger children may feel more vulnerable and show the distress by having trouble falling asleep, while older children may exhibit more attention problems in school. Sometimes children who initially show adjustment problems go on to adjust better than their older siblings.

How a child deals with divorce and the disrupted relationships in part depends on how secure their attachments are. However, other issues can also be relevant, such as income level, peer relationships, and the skills of the parents — especially the available parent. Divorce involving young children can be more disruptive to attachment than to older children.

On a more positive note, the decreasing stigma of divorce — in earlier times associated with social isolation, failure, and shame — makes adjustment, while difficult in itself, somewhat less stressful.

ENCOURAGING AND PROTECTING ATTACHMENT

There is no "cookbook" or "formula" for how to encourage and protect attachment between you and your child. Divorce often brings disrupted parent-child relationships, decreased social support, and increased stress, anxiety, and depression. Research shows that these disruptions with parents can affect children and interfere with their child developing strong positive attachment. Repeated observation of child behavioral problems should lead the parent to professional consultation about the situation.

As for the children, research tends to show that the most socially skilled youth typically have had parents who provided a sense of security when they were little. The fostering and maintenance of secure attachment can encourage stable intimate relationships for children when they mature into adults.

During and following divorce, be mindful of attachment. Neither parent should attempt to disrupt the child's existing attachment to the other parent. Such disruption can be very detrimental to the child's emotional development and can cause confusion and a sense of loss that can have lasting negative consequences.

Long gaps in parent-child contact can be detrimental to parent-child relationships, including being disruptive to attachment. Fostering regularity and predictability is always important in relationships, even more so during divorce and post-divorce when frequency of contact often is reduced.

Keeping all appointments for contact with your child is important, as is being on time. Children may experience anxiety following disruptions and unpredictability.

Fostering an even-tempered environment with regularity and predictability and absent unruly intensity, anger, and yelling also is important. Children — especially young ones — do best with regularity and predictability during visits, which is also constructive to attachment.

TAKEAWAYS

Children who feel safe and cared for from the start are likely to handle the disruption of divorce better than those who do not have dependable attachment figures. During and after divorce, children need continuity in those emotional bonds.

Notes

Notes

CHAPTER

7

IMPACT: DOMESTIC VIOLENCE

T he term "domestic violence" most often refers to acts of violence between established partners: marital, cohabiting non-married, non-cohabiting, dating, and — sometimes — former. "Family violence" refers to child maltreatment or abuse, sibling abuse, and elder abuse.

Behaviors that fall under the domestic violence category are defined legally in all states. From a behavioral standpoint, domestic violence is not a singular concept or syndrome with universal mechanisms and causes. It is complex, with many origins and triggers. Domestic violence is observed in all races, ethnicities, religions, and socioeconomic levels.

The U.S. Department of Justice National Crime Victimization Survey of 2015 indicates that the number of incidents of domestic violence — intimate partner violence — has recently increased. About 12 percent of simple and aggravated assaults were committed by intimate partners, most of which involved estranged partners, ex-spouses, and individuals in a dating relationship.

The impact of domestic violence on adults and involved children varies with different types of violence. External resources and internal resilience, as well as the degree of chronicity of the abuse, appear to be important, though researchers are still studying the components. The effects of domestic violence are broadly negative rather than positive, problematic rather than constructive, and usually debilitating rather than empowering.

Stalking crimes, related to domestic violence, most often are committed by estranged male partners or boyfriends against women who have terminated the relationship. Stalking often escalates, frequently necessitating the involvement of police and the legal system.

Formal statistics track domestic violence involving physical abuse. But emotional abuse is another form of domestic violence. Belittling, demeaning, intentional shaming, name calling, withholding money, flaunting infidelity, threatening to take the children away, and related provocative but not physically violent behaviors can take extreme tolls on victims.

While most research has focused on male perpetrators, there has been increasing study of female perpetrators in recent years. Straight as well as gay partner relationships also are being examined more.

IMPACT ON CHILDREN

Children who are involved in co-parenting disputes often experience stress and confusion. Such stress increases when domestic violence has been involved. Research into the impact of domestic violence on children often takes into account that children observe, hear, or overhear violence and get pulled into adult issues. This, of course, is problematic. Children need to be protected from adult conflicts and problematic behaviors so that they can focus on the normal challenges of childhood.

In general, younger children compared to older children experience a greater risk of negative effects from witnessing parental violence. Some research indicates that the more aware a child is of parental violence, the greater the contribution to emotional distress. Children living in residences with domestic violence experience increased risk of emotional and behavioral problems, including heightened fear and anger. Some studies report a decrease in attention and concentration affecting intellectual and academic functioning in school. Children can also be distracted and preoccupied by the problems of their parents instead of focusing on schoolwork and school relationships. Some research also indicates impaired social competence for children exposed to domestic violence. And a child in an abusive household is often secretive about the situation and can be reluctant to bring peers home.

Children who show resilience to the impact of exposure to domestic violence often have an independent, caring adult who is not in the home; some may have access to community resources that they may view as a sort of safe haven. Children of average to above-average intelligence level or who have positive self-esteem seem to be more resilient.

LEGAL INTERVENTION

There has been an increasing awareness by judges regarding domestic violence. Most judges in divorce cases consider spousal abuse to be significant and negative — and an important factor in making child custody determinations. Also, most states' custody statutes specifically cite domestic violence as a factor to be considered in making custody determinations. In fact, all 50 states have statutes focused on the standard of the best interests of the child.

Supervised parenting time can be an outcome in domestic violence matters, especially if the violence comes in the context of a child custody dispute. Termination of parental rights is infrequent, but possible. Involvement of Child Protective Services agencies is common. Sometimes courts rule on the failure of the non-abusing parent to protect the child against the abuser. Courts often mandate psychological treatment or abuser participation in remedial programs.

When abusive individuals use child visitation to gain access to the domestic violence victim or to retaliate, courts often appoint a professional monitor to directly work with the parties on a frequent basis, performing mediation-like services. The focus is on fostering cooperation in the best interests of the child.

Sometimes shelters or safe houses that allow no interaction with the alleged abuser are utilized in domestic violence situations. The first American domestic violence shelter was founded in the 1960s, and now there are thousands.

As for legal interventions regarding domestic violence, a Personal Protection Order (PPO), also known as a No Contact or Restraining Order, can be an injunction to prevent contact of any kind between two people (the focus typically being more on one person than the other). Even when PPOs are obtained, they are not always followed, and judges and the court referees who stand in for judges can vary in the degree of enforcement. Since human behavior is generally guided by its consequences, this can be a significant problem. Abusers who learn they can sometimes avoid consequences feel empowered to continue the abuse.

Sometimes these prohibitions extend to social media and the internet. There are occasions when one spouse posts derogatory or demeaning pictures or hurtful statements on Facebook, YouTube, or other sites. Revenge porn is the placement online of compromising photos or videos of a former partner, often featuring nudity and sexual situations. The court may rule that there is to be no further such posting and will impose penalties with violations.

SOME QUESTIONS TO CONSIDER REGARDING POTENTIAL PHYSICAL PARTNER/SPOUSE ABUSE:
- Was there physical violence in your family?
- Have you or your partner ever hit each other?
- Have you or your partner ever threatened to hit or kill each other, your children, or friends and family?
- During conflicts, do you or your partner threaten anyone's safety, break things, throw objects, punch walls, slam doors, ignore the other partner, or leave?
- Have you or your partner ever shoved, grabbed, hit, slapped, or choked the other, or any past partners?
- Do you or your partner tend to blame others for your behavior — especially your partner?

POWER & CONTROL WHEEL

PHYSICAL VIOLENCE

SEXUAL VIOLENCE

Power & Control

Using Coercion and Threats
· Threats are statements that promise negative consequences for certain behaviors or actions. For example, "I'll kill you if you ever leave me." · Coercion is a statement or action that implies, indirectly, negative or positive consequences for certain behaviors or actions. For example, cleaning the house and buying flowers the day after abuse.

Using Intimidation
· Making her afraid by using looks, actions, gestures, intoxication, "silent treatment." · Smashing things. · Destroying property. · Harming pets. · Displaying weapons. · Yelling. · Stalking her. · Slamming doors. · Driving recklessly. · Acting "crazy," invincible, or like "I have nothing to lose."

Using Economic Abuse
· Concealing or denying information about finances. · Using family/her assets without her knowledge or permission. · Preventing her from getting, keeping or leaving a job. · Damaging her credit rating. · Making her ask for money. · Destroying checkbooks, credit cards, money, or property. · Giving her an allowance.

Using Emotional Abuse
· Putting her down. · Making her feel bad about herself. · Calling her names. · Making her think she's crazy. · Playing mind games · Humiliating her. · Making her feel guilty. · Using things that matter to her against her. · Negatively comparing her to others. · Unreasonable demands or expectations. · Honeymooning her. · Perfectionism.

Using Male Privilege
· Defining what men's and women's roles are. · Defining what is and isn't "important." · Controlling the decision-making process. · Making and enforcing self-serving rules. · Treating her as an inferior. · Acting like the "master of the castle." · Believing or saying, "It's my right as a man to behave this way." · Acting like God.

Using Others
· Using the children to relay messages. · Using visitation to harass her. · Threatening to take the children away. · Using custody of the children as leverage. · Abusing the children. · Sexual abuse of the children. · Kidnapping the children. · Degrading her about her relationships. · Using her job, family, friends, religion, etc. as leverage.

Using Obfuscation
· Denying or minimizing the existence, severity, or impact of abusive behavior. · Blaming or otherwise shifting responsibility for abusive behavior. · Lying about, concealing, withholding, or omitting information, situations, or behavior to gain advantage. · Pretending to be a victim to gain sympathy, support, or allies. · Using intoxication as an excuse.

Using Isolation
· Controlling her access to resources such as birth control, reproductive choices, medical attention, money, education, employment opportunities, family friends, transportation, phone use. · Using jealousy to justify actions. · Embarrassing her in front of others. · Kidnapping her. · Convincing her that seeing her family or friends is "harmful to our relationship."

- Do you try to control how your partner thinks and/or dresses, whom they see, and how they spend time or money?
- Do you threaten to hurt your partner, yourself, or others if they talk about leaving you?
- Is your partner afraid of you sometimes?
- Are you or your partner cruel to animals?
- Do you or your partner abuse alcohol or other drugs?

SOME QUESTIONS TO CONSIDER REGARDING EMOTIONAL PARTNER/SPOUSE ABUSE:

- Do you or your partner think that everyone treats him or her badly?
- Are you or your partner preoccupied with "getting even" or "getting back"?
- Are you or your partner very jealous or possessive? Have you been told that?
- Do you or your partner drive friends and family away or put a wedge between you and them?
- Do you or your partner treat the other as personal property and expect the other to anticipate your needs?
- Do you or your partner demonstrate significant mood swings?
- Do you or your partner threaten suicide if the partner leaves?

If you recognize yourself or your partner in affirmative answers to one or more of these questions, consider getting help. You can identify and contact local skilled treatment professionals, and you can contact the organizations that follow as a first step.

FALSE ALLEGATIONS

The frequency of false allegations of domestic violence may be higher in custody and parenting time cases than in other circumstances. A partner could potentially think he or she could gain from asserting false allegations of domestic violence. Such assertions could potentially be a ploy.

However, there can be significant negative consequences to the accuser if it's determined that domestic violence allegations have been contrived and intentionally false.

If you are the subject of such a false allegation, it would seem important to consider immediately retaining a skilled and experienced defense attorney. This particularly would be urgent if the police or a child protective agency is involved. Do not delay. Act immediately.

TAKEAWAYS

Domestic violence affects everyone in a family and is taken seriously by judges. Sometimes a partner seeks a Personal Protection Order or must go to a shelter for self-protection and for the safety of their children. Perpetrators should seek help.

NEED HELP?

Many states have local helplines you can contact. Below are examples of some national domestic violence organization resources.

˙National Domestic Violence Hotline
800/799-SAFE (7233) : *thehotline.org*

˙National Coalition Against Domestic Violence
303/839-1852 : *ncadv.org*

˙Safe Horizon
800/621-HOPE (4673) : *safehorizon.org*

˙Rape, Abuse & Incest National Network
800/656-HOPE (4673) : *rainn.org*

˙Stalking Resource Center of the National Center for Victims of Crime
202/467-8700 : *victimsofcrime.org*

˙Connection to a Crisis Counselor
In U.S. text 741741 : *crisistextline.org*

• • •

Notes

Notes

CHAPTER 8

ALCOHOL AND BEYOND:
HOW SUBSTANCE ABUSE AFFECTS CUSTODY

S

ubstance abuse is a major problem in our society and a frequent factor in divorce. Alcohol has always been a huge issue in many child custody and parenting time cases.

Now we are undergoing an epidemic of opiate addiction and deaths due to overdoses. Some experts consider it to be the greatest drug epidemic this country has ever experienced. Countless lives are being destroyed and marriages ruined.

While marijuana is going through a huge transformation, becoming legal for recreational use in numerous states including Michigan, California, and Colorado and available in most states for medicinal purposes, it could still be a factor in divorce proceedings. It's also important to know that marijuana and marijuana-related products are much more potent than they were 15 or 20 years ago.

ALCOHOLISM

Too often ignored, alcoholism is a major problem in our society. Consider a case in which a client was pulled over for drinking with an open alcohol container while driving on a highway with her children in the car. She was charged with driving while intoxicated and lost custody of her children. In that situation, she was ordered into an alcohol treatment program and had supervised parenting time with her children for an extended period of time.

In other cases, alcohol addiction has played a major role in not only whether a parent should have custody of the children, but also whether he or she should even see the children except on a limited or supervised basis.

An alcoholic is someone who relies on alcohol. He or she can be a binge drinker or someone who consumes alcohol on a daily basis. People will often say that there is nothing wrong with a couple of drinks every day. That may be the case, but it depends upon the person and whether he or she is dependent on those daily drinks. The key is whether this will affect parenting ability. It can be a major factor in any custody dispute.

Many clients are functioning alcoholics. That means they can go about their daily routines, but at the end of the day, will have problems. We have seen many situations where a party to a case comes home from work and has a few beers or shots, and then lies down on the couch until bedtime. These clearly become issues in a custody case.

Many alcoholics are in total denial until there is a significant and debilitating problem — rock bottom — and life for the person feels like a disaster from which they may feel they cannot recover. In some situations, with women more than men, there have been allegations that they are secret alcoholics who go about their routine each day but are often near a bottle of wine that becomes a crutch for daily living. Often, stores of alcohol are secreted in closets, kitchen cabinets, and other hiding places throughout the home; the other party is not fully aware because the drinking is done while one parent is alone in the house.

These issues can heavily influence a custody case, especially when the drinking affects a parent's ability to fully watch and care for children. In one case, the father was an alcoholic, and was not properly supervising children while they were swimming. He was drunk and the children almost drowned.

In preparing a custody case, it is important to look into someone's driving record. Have there been issues regarding driving while impaired or other substance abuse problems?

OPIATES/OPIOIDS

Opiate addiction has a tremendous impact on custody and parenting time cases. We have worked together on cases where one parent could not function without his or her daily supply of opiates. In some situations, this affected the parent's ability to wake up and get the children to school or to be there when they returned. When a parent sleeps through much of the day, taking care of children — let alone himself or herself — is an impossibility.

What is an opiate? It is defined as a drug with morphine-like effects, derived from opium. Synonyms include sedatives, tranquilizers, depressants, and anesthetics. Sadly, they fill almost everyone's medicine cabinets and are too readily available by prescription. In 2014, 259 million prescriptions for opioids were written — almost one for every American!

Opiates are a multibillion-dollar industry with the pharmaceutical companies as well as our medical communities. The billion-dollar profit received by Big

Pharma has resulted in billions of dollars in legal expenses, prisons, treatment, and the destruction of many lives and families. There is a tremendous impact on law enforcement as well as on custody and parenting time.

Over the years, we have seen many cases where alcohol and drugs such as heroin or cocaine were factors in the breakdown of a marriage as well as regarding the custody of the children in both marital and nonmarital relationships. In recent years, we have seen more and more cases where the issues were over addiction to prescription drugs including antidepressants and Oxycontin, hydrocodone, gabapentin, Xanax, alprazolam, and other highly addictive and dangerous opioids and benzodiazepines.

Years ago, a close doctor friend had refused to fill a prescription for Vicodin with the result that the patient — clearly an addict — came back to his office, attacked, and almost killed him. The doctor was hospitalized for days. After a criminal trial, the addict ended up spending several years in prison for criminal assault.

The impact upon the custody of your children can be tremendous. We have dealt with cases where the mother of the children was going to numerous pharmacies for opiates, due to her chronic back pain. In one case, a client was able to obtain a prescription pad and wrote numerous prescription refills. Doctors running opioid mills and the sale of opioids on the street have become all too common. Thankfully, as this book is being written, there are much tighter regulations on prescriptions.

In these situations, it is common to subpoena the various pharmacies to get a history of the prescriptions, their frequency, and amount. This information can be critical in determining custody or parenting time where someone is clearly addicted.

We have had cases where custody of the children was lost due to the issue of opiate addiction. Parenting time can be greatly restricted or supervised as well where there is a serious addiction problem.

The courts and legal system are beginning to understand the severity of the opiate epidemic and its impact upon the family.

While we deal with issues involving alcohol all of the time, we need to be more aware of the dangerous and addictive nature of opiates/opioids and other addictive drugs.

MARIJUANA

Marijuana may be legal and regulated in some states, but it is still a controlled substance that is illegal at the federal level. Marijuana use can be very tricky in general — and especially when it comes to the custody of your children.

What are the courts doing about the issue of medical marijuana and marijuana in general? If it is legal either as a recreational drug or for medical purposes, most courts will treat it like they would alcohol or other addictive drugs.

A lot is going to depend on your state and how conservative or liberal the laws and judges are regarding this issue. In more liberal jurisdictions, the issue will be looked at based on the impact on the children and their best interests. Many judges have the attitude that there is to be no marijuana smoked or ingested when a parent has the children in his or her custody for parenting time purposes. For example, if there is a split custodial arrangement, it could mean that when you have the children, you can't smoke or use marijuana products. If you are high, it is similar to the consequences for being drunk or high on other opiates or drugs and becomes a basis for having limited contact with your children.

When it comes to marijuana, alcohol, opiates, or other drugs, it is critical to discuss these in-depth with your attorney and to be fully honest if any are an issue. This can be critical regarding what is in the best interests of your children and can have a profound effect on custody and parenting time.

 ....

WHAT TO LOOK FOR

Following are a few things to think about regarding the care and custody of children in relation to substance abuse.

1. Do you know what is in your medicine cabinet? Often people will store potent prescriptions even though the need for them has ended. Seventy percent of illicit drugs that our children use come from a family member or a family member's medicine cabinet.

2. Are you getting rid of prescription painkillers if they are no longer needed? Think of cold remedies and medications such as cough syrup with codeine. These can be addictive. Prescriptions have expiration dates and should not be kept forever. If they are kept, use a prescription safe.

3. We have dealt with situations where children have gone through their parents' medicine cabinets and taken their finds to parties or friends' homes where all of the pills are tossed into a bowl. These are called "pharm parties." The kids will then start grabbing and ingesting them at random without knowing what they are. The results can be tragic — overdose and even death! Make sure prescription medications are not accessible.

4. Do you know what pills are in the house and whether they are accessible to your children?

5. If your spouse or the parent of your child may have a problem with prescription drugs, do not ignore it. Does he or she need drugs every day to function? Is he or she excessively sleeping? Is he or she constantly seeking prescription refills? Are there changes in behavior patterns or personality? Is he or she constantly complaining of chronic pain? It could be a significant

issue in a custody or parenting time dispute. This is where a subpoena of medical or pharmaceutical records can be critical.

6. If there is a settlement and addiction is an issue, it is important to insist on regular testing at a clinic or facility that specializes in this type of drug testing.

7. Counseling can be an important part of the equation, as can a drug treatment or rehab program when the problem is serious.

8. Opiate addiction not only can lead to a custody battle or divorce, but also can involve criminal behavior.

9. Some warning signs of a drug problem can include a spouse or significant other who is always taking medications. Examples include sleeping a lot more than normal and not being up to get the children off to school or to put them to bed at night. Is he or she always complaining about chronic pain? Was there an accident that required drugs as part of the treatment where the time for full recovery has long passed and yet the parent continues to seek prescriptions and complain of chronic pain? These are all signs of a possible addiction.

10. If you are concerned that your child is having a problem with opiates or other drugs, seek help immediately. The consequences of denial can be tragic.

•••

TAKEAWAYS

Significant issues regarding custody and parenting time include dealing with addiction and the impact of alcohol, opiates, marijuana, and other drugs. These are a major issue in our society and cannot be ignored. Having a problem with addiction can mean the difference between maintaining and losing custody of your children.

Notes

CHAPTER

9

SOCIAL MEDIA & TECHNOLOGY

Facebook and other social media sites have become a growing and significant factor in the breakup of marriages and other relationships. We now have public figures and even the President of the United States tweeting on a regular basis. Without thinking, it is so easy to push a button on your computer, smartphone, or tablet and expose some of your most personal issues to the entire world.

People now don't communicate primarily by phone or the US Mail but, far more typically, do so electronically — by text, email, or Facebook, for example.

Take a case involving Twitter vs. the First Amendment. Former NBA great Steve Nash and his former wife had a joint custody agreement including a non-disparagement clause. This meant that they had to communicate in a respectful fashion, which should be the goal of all couples regarding their children. In this case, the former wife made inappropriate tweets about Nash. The court barred her from making any further disparaging comments on social media about him.

She argued that this violated her First Amendment right to freedom of speech. The appellate court upheld the non-disparagement order. In its ruling, the court stated that because Nash was a well-known athlete, comments about him on social media are highly visible and could be harmful if seen by their children.

A key issue with regard to the custody of children is the fact that the courts now focus on the availability of postings on Facebook for a child's possible observation. You don't have to prove that your child actually saw the postings.

It's not uncommon — and a very bad idea — for one of the parties in a divorce to post Facebook pictures of boyfriends or girlfriends in the middle of the proceedings.

Other examples include a case in Indiana where sexually explicit Facebook posts made between a mother and her boyfriend were discovered. She argued that the posts were deleted, and there was no evidence the children saw them. The posts were still allowed into evidence at trial because of the possibility the children could see them.

If you are going through a divorce or custody battle, it is critical to be careful regarding your use of Facebook and other forms of social media. Once you post something on Facebook, it is potentially available for the entire world to see. If the photos are compromising or show a lack of discretion, this could have an effect on your custody or parenting time battle.

Do not post and do not text. Text messages can be critical in a court hearing or trial. We have had numerous cases where angry or incriminating text messages have become part of the court record as evidence.

Compromising videos and photos that are shot during a relationship or marriage can come back to haunt you, especially if they are posted online. Ask Jeff Bezos and other celebrities.

There are so many other issues where the internet can come into play in a custody battle. Consider the following:

1. Online gambling, which can represent a form of compulsive behavior or even addiction, can have an impact on the outcome of a custody dispute.
2. Viewing pornography online can become a custody-related issue. In a recent case, after the divorce was finalized, the former husband was with his girlfriend. The girlfriend's child was in another bedroom showing internet porn to his younger children. This became a major issue, with repercussions for the children.
3. People often meet online and have internet affairs. In one case where the custody of the children was a major issue, in the middle of the divorce and through the internet, one ex-spouse reignited an old high school romance with someone who lived thousands of miles away. The ex-spouse left the children and moved in with the old flame. This resulted in the other parent getting custody. No doubt we all have heard of similar situations.
4. We have had cases where children have become obsessed with playing video games, with the result that they had to drop out of school and receive intensive inpatient treatment for their obsession.

MAINTAIN YOUR PRIVACY

We live in a world where computers are frequently hacked. If you are worried that your computer is being hacked, talk to your attorney in person. Experts can be hired to check your computers to make sure that they have not been compromised by spyware, malware, or other monitoring software. Also, change your passwords.

If you are concerned about privacy, talk to your attorney in person and not by phone or email. Do not say or post anything that could come back to haunt you. Never post compromising pictures on the internet.

Stop and think twice before you say or do anything. There are many ways that you may be taped or compromised in this cyber age.

With smartphones, there are often family plans. These can become tracking devices so that your spouse or significant other can monitor you and know where you are at any given time. When privacy is a concern, these plans should be separated and partners should get their own accounts. The array of devices for surveillance is endless. They include hidden cameras, spyware, keystroke monitors, GPS tracking devices, drones, and voice recorders, among others.

There are even "smart" mattresses available that indicate when an individual is present in the bed.

WHAT'S LEGAL?

The laws regulating these devices vary from state to state. It is important to discuss these issues with your attorney in a custody or parenting time dispute, and to follow the laws of your state.

For example, Michigan is a one-person state regarding phone conversations. This means you can tape the conversation even if the person you are speaking with is unaware of it. However, you must be part of the conversation. In many states, both parties must be aware the conversation is being taped. If they are not, it may be illegal.

Can you tape your children's conversations? If you are not on the phone, most likely the answer is no.

Computer spyware such as keystroking and other devices are illegal everywhere. GPS tracking devices can be legal in some states and not in others. In Michigan, it is now illegal for an individual to place such a device on a car he or she doesn't own. If you co-own the vehicle, it is still OK. On the other hand, a licensed private investigator can use a GPS tracking device, as can a law enforcement officer. Have your attorney check the laws in your state if this becomes an issue.

GPS trackers can pinpoint a location. They can show someone's entire route from beginning to end. They can detail activity reports. They can show arrival from a specific address as well as departure from an address. They can provide notification if a vehicle moves — and if it doesn't move by a pre-defined time. They can operate at odd hours.

Plenty of iPhone apps can become important in a custody battle. Apple Voice Memos turns your phone into an audio recording device.

Find My Friends is an app that allows you to share your location or view other people's locations. You can hide from your friends on the app at any time with the Hide My Location feature.

Find My iPhone allows for remote location-tracking of iPhones, iPads, and

Mac computers. Any person with this information can view your location from any computer, cell phone, or other web-based device. To make sure that you aren't being tracked, either change your login information regularly or turn off Find My iPhone.

Android and browser apps include some of the following: Divorce Log, *2houses. com*, Custody Junction, Online Parenting Time Information Manager and Activity Log, and Android Device Manager (locates and erases your Android device).

The technology and possibilities are changing so rapidly that as this is being written, there are numerous changes being made. The law is clearly lagging behind a lot of the latest technology.

If email is on a family computer, it can be fair game if it is open. If it is on a separate computer, going into an email account can be in violation of the law.

If you are concerned about compromising photos that may be on the internet, search for yourself on Google to see if any pictures appear. If the posting of a picture can be traced to the other parent in a custody case, this may be indicative of this individual's behavior and ability to parent.

Electronic evidence can be very important in a custody trial or hearing. Examples include email accounts and messages, social networking accounts, text messages and chatroom conversations, website content and postings, digital photographs, computer-stored records, and data.

For example, a mother's parental rights were terminated after evidence revealed she had been soliciting prostitution on a website. The evidence was allowed because of testimony from a witness confirming that the mother corresponded directly with her on the website. The evidence was relevant because it went directly to the issue of her fitness as a parent.

As for spy cameras and drones, the law is continually evolving. However, the general rule is that if the devices are in a public area where there is no expectation of privacy, then they are OK. For example, spyware in a living room, family room, kitchen, or a backyard or deck would be legal. In a bedroom or bathroom, where there is an expectation of privacy, it would be illegal.

In one custody case, a hidden camera recorded a parent having sex in the family room. There was also a young child who happened to walk by and was caught on camera as well. That could have destroyed the client's custody chances but for the fact that the child was her paramour's offspring — not hers.

The facts of every case are extremely important. No two cases are alike.

These are all issues that you should discuss with your attorney as you go forward with a case involving the custody of your children. Yes, it's all subject to rules of evidence, which means that they must be relevant to your case and also must be authenticated. It is easy to fabricate pictures and even texts or emails. These can be technical issues where it is critical that your attorney understands technology and the applicable rules of evidence.

But in this age of technology and social media, nothing is safe. There is every reason to be wary and careful as you go through a custody or parenting time dispute. It is critical that you discuss these issues with your attorney and/or psychotherapist.

TAKEAWAYS

We are in an age of social media where the internet, electronic devices, spyware, drones, and other technology can have an impact on child custody cases. Talk to your attorney and psychotherapist for advice — and by all means, be careful in dealing with the other parent.

Notes

_____

_____

_____

_____

_____

_____

_____

_____

_____

_____

_____

_____

_____

_____

_____

_____

_____

_____

_____

_____

_____

_____

_____

_____

_____

_____

CHAPTER 10

CULTURAL ISSUES

As we write *Child Custody*, we are seeing an even greater impact of cultural, religious, and ethnic issues because of the division in our country over immigration and citizenship rights. As a result, some people feel unsettled, uncertain, angry, and even frightened.

We live in complex and uncertain times. This is clearly affecting nuclear families. We have seen many cases involving Green Cards, student visas, and other immigration issues that have an effect on custodial arrangements. This complex area of child custody and immigration issues often overlap.

The metropolitan Detroit area is diverse, with many ethnic and religious communities. We have a very large Islamic community, and strong Jewish representation along with other religious and ethnic groups. Thousands are Hispanic. Many are from India or Pakistan, Russia, Eastern Europe, or Asia. Many religious traditions are represented.

The Detroit area also has a large Italian influence, as well as Irish and the British Isles. We also have a large African-American population. The Detroit area clearly represents the increasingly dynamic diverse culture of the United States. That means we are seeing many custody battles involving people from foreign lands with different belief systems and cultures.

IMPACT OF ETHNIC BACKGROUND

As an attorney and as a psychologist, we know that it is important to examine the differences and try to learn from them, since cultural background influences behavior and values. When first meeting with a client, a goal is not only to gather information about the custody issues, but also to become familiar with any cultural factors that might have an effect on custody and parenting time issues.

For example, if a parent disappears with a child to certain countries in the Middle East, as well as to some other parts of the world that are not signatories to the Hague Convention regarding international child abduction, there is no reciprocity and it is impossible to have a child returned if the absent parent refuses.

The female role in the Middle East and much of Asia can differ greatly from that in the United States. In some cultures, women are still expected to remain in the home and defer to their husbands; they may not be active in the community or hold employment. We have also had many clients where in-laws from a foreign country move in and take over the childrearing or create constant conflict with a daughter- or son-in-law.

It is more and more common for people to marry into other faiths. So if the marriage or nonmarital relationship breaks down, the religious upbringing of the children can become a battleground.

It is not unusual for a husband or wife who converted from Catholicism to Judaism to return to Catholicism when the marriage ends. This can happen with many religions, leading to battles over holidays and parenting time. Some cases have involved disputes about parenting time and holidays in different branches of Judaism. In some cases where parents are members of the same religion, they cannot agree on which church, synagogue, mosque, or temple the children should attend. In one case, a rabbi was called as a witness to testify as to which holidays were the most important for visitation/parenting time purposes.

We have been involved in many complicated and hard-fought custody battles where both parents feel that they are capable of and entitled to joint legal and physical custody. As an attorney and a psychotherapist, we know it is important to listen to clients and try to understand their background and its implications. These extremely sensitive issues must be recognized and considered carefully when determining the best strategy for each client. Every case is unique and deserves a different approach. Extra attention can result in a more satisfied client.

ISSUES TO ANTICIPATE

As an example, in a marriage of over a decade, a wife was told by her husband to get out with their three children. She then filed for a divorce only to learn through the response filed by her husband's attorney that they had never been legally married. They had gone through an Islamic marriage ceremony, but for some reason the license was never properly recorded — hence, no marriage.

Such cases often turn into issues involving custody and parenting time. In addition, civil actions often are filed on behalf of one spouse, based upon fraud, unjust enrichment, and misrepresentations on the part of the other spouse. In the example above, since they were not legally married, another legal basis had to be determined, as there is no common law marriage in Michigan nor in most other states. The ultimate result of the dilemma was that the "wife" recovered monetary damages as well as custody of the three children.

As an attorney and psychologist, we see many unusual situations with people who are unfamiliar with our culture and laws. In many countries, grandparents, aunts, and uncles live together as one big "happy family." This can create problems for someone who is not used to this. In many families, a lot of the childrearing is done by grandparents. These are all issues that must be recognized in any custody case where culture becomes an issue.

We have talked with rabbis and other various religious clergy about the fact that long after a divorce, paternity suit, or custody case has concluded, the parents can continue to battle. Members of the faith will be counseling parishioners on such issues as baptism, bar and bat mitzvahs, communions, confirmations, and other religious occasions. There can be arguments over who can participate, who is to be invited, and even whether an actual parent should be included when he or she is not a member of the same faith. These are all issues that can fester for years through the court system.

With the turmoil that our country is undergoing and, sadly, with a lack of tolerance by many for people who are of a different race, creed, or religion, these are all issues that will be raising their ugly heads more and more frequently.

Following are some observations from a judge whom we highly respect and who has an excellent reputation. This judge is of the Islamic faith. Several years ago, she started wearing a hijab; her religion is important to her and covering her head is a symbol of purity.

On any given day, there typically are many other members of the Islamic faith in her courtroom, as well as other litigants representing other religious, racial, and ethnic backgrounds who are dealing with custody or other family law matters.

She explained that she gives people time and listens because cultures can vary considerably in determining how people express themselves. For example, one couple from Africa in her court was very loud while speaking. By letting them proceed in that manner, she made it possible for them to communicate in a way that may have been culturally normal to them, though atypical to us. She realized that listening and trying to account for cultural, religious, racial, and ethnic differences improves the process and leads to better understanding. This is very important in family law matters such as child custody.

TAKEAWAYS

It is important for clients from a foreign country or distinct cultural background to make sure that their attorney is sensitive to the intricacies of custody and parenting time disputes where cultural or ethnic considerations come into play. Everyone is a product of their environment, and our cultural and ethnic identities can mean a great deal to us. The exact same set of circumstances can be interpreted in a variety of ways, depending on the client's heritage and background. An attorney, evaluator, or psychotherapist must not only be knowledgeable, but also compassionate and focused on satisfying the specific needs of the client during the difficult time of a custody or parenting time dispute.

Notes

Notes

_____

_____

_____

_____

_____

_____

_____

_____

_____

_____

_____

_____

_____

_____

_____

_____

_____

_____

_____

_____

_____

_____

_____

_____

_____

_____

CHAPTER 11

PARENTAL ALIENATION

Post-relationship separation for both married and non-married couples typically has a significant effect on children. The separation process and the aftermath can be difficult for both parents and kids.

When partners, whether married or not, no longer cohabit and there is a child or children involved, less time is spent between each parent and the child — sometimes dramatically less.

The actual move-out process can in itself be upsetting, and children should be protected from that experience if possible. Sometimes thing go awry. Also, after parental separation, sometimes negative thoughts and emotions are expressed by one or both parents about the other. Sometimes these thoughts are intense, and expressed in hearing range of children. That experience, especially if repeated, can be stressful for a child. In a sense, it makes clear to the child that the two parents do not support each other. A child is likely to fear this may continue, and it sometimes does. It can be confusing and unintentionally call into question feelings of attachment of the child to the parent being spoken of negatively.

DISRUPTING RELATIONSHIPS

If a parent has been close to a child, that contact and involvement is disrupted when that parent moves out of the home. For that reason, it is often helpful to maintain regular and substantial contact as a way of minimizing stress for the child.

But sometimes conflicts escalate and alienation can disrupt that contact. The negative feelings of an estranged partner can get mixed in, especially if that parent lives with and has more access to the child. There may be a blending of bad feelings for the estranged partner with some parental anticipation or even expectation that the child should somehow recognize that the other parent is "no good," flawed, or antagonistic. This can be subtly or unintentionally communicated, or it can be intentionally communicated by a parent directly or indirectly.

The parent may feel justified and comfortable in denigrating the other parent. In whatever ways they are communicated, such viewpoints can be stressful to the child, producing anxiety and anger. They may come to identify with one parent and feel emotionally distant from the other. Often the alienating parent is reassuring to them, and the child may view the alienated parent as the cause of anxiety.

Children can come to feel that they should be loyal to and supportive of the negative-speaking parent, especially if they live with and spend more time with that parent. Of course, both parents can be negative speakers, which makes many children feel very vulnerable for being put in the middle when they are not interested in hearing negative statements — either direct or implied — by both parents. They have no "safe zone." They have little respite, since both environments contain antagonism and stress.

Sometimes a child may find it best (or simpler or more comfortable) to take sides. A child may experience anxiety at the increasing parental disharmony, at the prospect of the parents separating, and during their actual separation. The most stressful of these circumstances can lead to alienation of the child from one parent.

Sometimes children blame one parent or the other for the separation, in part to help reduce anxiety and uncertainty. The likelihood of this happening can depend to some degree on the nature of the child's prior relationship with each parent. Often, but not always, the closer the pre-separation parent-child relationship, the less likely it is that such alienation will occur.

However — and it is very difficult to ascertain — one parent may actively pursue alienation of the child to gain advantage in the parental separation. Although no parent will admit to or take responsibility for this, it can happen. Separating parents sometime may feel justified in doing this, though such parental behavior never is in the best interests of the child. Typically this is the worst of situations because it puts the most stress on the child.

RECOGNIZING ALIENATING BEHAVIORS

Alienated behavior involves rejection of the other parent. This can take many forms.

Such behavior by a child can be rooted in the relationship of the child with the estranged parent — or not. Many factors can be in play. If there has been physical violence, the child may feel one parent needs to be protected. Sometimes children align with the parent they feel is less strong or more needy. Sometimes the child may have legitimate fears or apprehensions toward a parent and the alienation may come from a history of a poor relationship. Sometimes a child overhears things about that parent, true or otherwise, and may form negative views.

The extent of reaction can vary. The child may not want to see or otherwise have contact with the other parent. The child may refuse contact directly. The child may become emotionally distant and impassive, giving minimal responses to one parent. Some go silent or isolate and stay in their rooms with little interaction. Sometimes these behaviors expand to include the parents and extended family of that parent, but not the parents and extended family of the non-alienated parent.

In some cases, alienated children explain their sudden change of attitude toward one parent as based on past mistakes or personality imperfections. The alienation from the relatives and extended family of the alienated parent is often based on even flimsier reasons, or no reason at all, and can be based on the grandparents, for example, being supportive of the alienated parent. It is not uncommon for alienated children to describe the alienated parent in the same terms as those used by the alienating parent.

The intensity and the length of time over which alienation develops varies. Generally, the more intense and long-lasting, the worse the damage to the parent-child relationship. Professional intervention may be wise, such as a psychotherapist trained and experienced in such situations. Often courts attempt to deal with that situation, with varying degrees of success. One thing courts can do is enforce consequences for not following court orders. Beyond that, courts cannot force solutions.

More than legal and judicial involvement, professional intervention can more often be most helpful. One of the most problematic scenarios is the playing out of alienation in a courtroom. Most courtroom situations are adversarial — not the best model in domestic disputes.

TAKEAWAYS

Parents can be helpful to their children and supportive of them if they examine their behavior and the effect it has on their child. The breakup of a relationship is a time of negative value judgments. Children should be sheltered as much as possible from participating.

ALIENATION Q&A

Q. What is Parental Alienation Syndrome (PAS)?

In 1970, a child psychiatrist named Richard Gardner wrote a popular and controversial book titled *The Boys and Girls Book About Divorce*. It discusses children who align with one parent in rejecting and denigrating the other parent, with that attitude typically extending to the family of the denigrated parent. Gardner coined the term Parent Alienation Syndrome (PAS). Since alienation is sometimes a part of divorce, the concept became useful and popular with lawyers and others working with families of divorce.

Gardner's concepts caused controversy for several reasons. While multiple factors are responsible for alienation, Gardner seemed to focus on mothers often being responsible for parental alienation. Also, readers often interpreted the recommendations as necessitating change of custody if PAS was found in a particular situation. And for those accused of PAS, it sometimes became difficult to prove a negative, to clearly demonstrate that they had not alienated the child(ren), since there already was so much intensity and strife.

One of the contributions of Gardner's book was that it called attention to the feelings of children in divorce. It also highlighted how divorce sometimes damages parent-child relationships. Over time, the syndrome aspect appears less clear and less coherent, and the circumstances and known dynamics of parental separation appear more complex. The most common term used now is parental alienation.

Q. If I am in a parental alienation situation, why shouldn't I "fight fire with fire" and become equally nasty back?

Think of what is likely to be effective and consider what the effect may be on your child. The matter can be dealt with in court, and the courts should enforce their orders.

Your primary focus should be on the relationship with your child. True, your child may be rude, uncaring, and obnoxious now, but they have not always been that way, and likely they will not be that way in the future. Although you may experience an impulse to retaliate and to treat the child as you have been treated, you are a role model. Do not argue with the child over the allegations. If the child does not look to you now, they may in the future, as they may have in the past.

You are responsible for your behavior. Examine your actions and see if you have anything to improve. The child may be looking for excuses to behave badly. Do not serve up those excuses. Expressions of anger and punishment may appear to validate to the child what the alienating parent has been saying about you. Also, voluntary abandonment by you, such as you refusing to visit the child, often is used as justification for the statements and behaviors of the child and alienating parent.

Try to view the situation from the child's perspective. If the intentional alienating dynamics are going on, children may be "in the middle" and "stuck" and they may be choosing what they feel is a better alternative for their psychological survival.

Q. What do I do when I am falsely accused?

It would depend on what the accusations entail. If there are legal implications to the accusations, such as physical or sexual abuse, for example, consultation with an attorney may be wise. It always seems ill advised to represent yourself as a non-lawyer when you are dealing in specialized adversarial situations with people who are lawyers.

It may be important to hire an attorney who is not a family member, but who is experienced in the issue of parental alienation. You want expertise and you want objectivity.

Given the stress of such a situation, if you are not in a supportive therapeutic relationship, it may be wise to consider consulting with a mental health professional skilled in understanding post-relationship dynamics and the dynamics of alienation.

Consider whether your child needs supportive professional help. Be careful to find a skilled psychotherapist who also is not a partisan or an advocate of some specific kind — a professional inclined toward or against finding parental alienation. You want to find a person who is independent and with whom your child can relate.

●●●

Notes

CHAPTER 12

NEVER-MARRIED PARENTS

People most often are attracted to others by appearance. Similarities of culture, ethnicity, education, interests, and behavioral characteristics such as humor also can form the basis for attraction.

Attraction can lead to relationships, including those of a romantic nature. This can lead to living together and sometimes to marriage. Individual circumstances account for what can happen.

Trust is also a major part of human relationships — and certainly the centerpiece of stable human relationships. Trust is the basis for sharing and openness, partnership and reciprocation.

Most contentious breakups can involve the fracture of trust between the participants. This is as true for never-married couples as it is for married couples, though with never-marrieds, the same depth of trust often has not developed as with those who are married. Both partners know the relationship usually can be dissolved just by separating — much simpler, unless there are children, when it often becomes not simple at all. Never-marrieds typically haven't completed the same amount of merging of financial, social, emotional, and work lives as their married counterparts.

TRENDS IN MARRIAGE, COHABITING, AND REPRODUCTION

In recent times, there has been an increasing diversity of living arrangements for couples. Fewer male-female couples marry, but now same-sex couples can marry, and also many more couples live together without marriage. Overall there has been a decline in the prevalence of the two married-parent family. There are many single parents. Also, overall, the number of children being born has been decreasing. There has been a general decline in having children in the context of relationships. As for marriage, a lot has changed.

For one, adults are marrying later in life. In 1960, the average woman was age 20 at first marriage and the average man was 23. In 2012, the average ages were 27 for women and 29 for men.

The numbers of adults who don't marry have significantly increased. In 1960, 18 percent of adults had always been single. In 2012, the percent had increased to 40. And this significant increase in never-married adults cuts across racial lines.

Since the mid-1980s, the marriage rate has decreased steadily, in recent years flattening out at fewer than seven marriages per thousand — less than half the rate in the years following World War II.

The number of Americans marrying peaked after World War II. In more recent times, the number of people marrying topped out at about 2.5 million per year in the mid-1980s. More recently, about 2 million per year marry, even though the population continues to increase.

Currently about half the adults in the U.S. live with a spouse, also a significant decrease from 30 years ago. Even the recent rise of same-sex marriages has not counterbalanced the decline in heterosexual marriages.

Meanwhile, cohabitation has increased. In 1970, the rate of unmarried cohabitation was about one in 200 adults. Current figures are about 15 times that — about 7.5 percent.

There are numerous explanations for why fewer people marry and instead choose to live together without marriage. Economics is often cited. It may be more economical to live together than as a single person, but it is not more economical to marry.

Others say that women's increasing levels of education, income, and autonomy have contributed to the trends. More women are oriented to live independent lives than a few decades ago. Declining religious participation and beliefs have also been cited. It may be that each of these factors contributes.

THE FAMILY PICTURE

Traditionally in the U.S., families had two parents in the framework of marriage. In 1960, 72 percent of families were so structured. That's a contrast to 1990, when 58 percent of families had two parents married to each other, and to 2014, when the number declined to 50 percent.

The divorce rate during this time period increased substantially. Recent statistics show that between 40 and 50 percent of marriages end in divorce, though the divorce rate has been declining slightly.

In 1960, 5 percent of the adult population was living as separated or divorced. In 1990, the number was 11 percent, and now 14 percent of people are unattached.

Additionally, the percentage of people who have never married has increased from 15 percent in 1960 to 23 percent in 1990 to 30 percent in 2014. The number of adults currently separated, divorced, and never married approaches half the adult population. Even if you add recent married numbers to cohabitation numbers, the number of people together one way or the other has declined.

Another factor contributing to the changing structure of the American family has been the increasing number of two-parent families in which both parents work outside of the home. Currently both parents work full time in about half of two-parent households, with others where one parent may work part time. In 1970, 30 percent of families had both parents working full time.

Multigenerational households — those having three or more generations — have also been on the rise. An example of such a household would be one in which one or both grandparents reside, one of their offspring (with or without a partner), and one or more grandchildren. There are, of course, all sorts of variants.

In 1980, about 12 percent of households were multigenerational. Ten years ago, it was about 15 percent; now more than 18 percent of households are multigenerational. This marks a reverse of a prior trend of decreasing multigenerational family living over an approximate 50-year period.

NEVER-MARRIED VS. MARRIED

What follows are generalizations. Every person and couple is different.

First of all, many never-married couples with children stay together for a long time. Some eventually marry; others don't. Overall, never-married parents are more likely to break up than those who are married. The divorce rate for marrieds is 3.2 per 1,000 persons. The break-up rate is higher for never-marrieds, though formal statistics are harder to validate.

It is often the case for never-marrieds that there is less pressure to stay together. There tends to be less support for both parties from their extended family than if they were married. Grandparents or siblings of the never-marrieds may not feel as invested or be as involved as the corresponding relatives for marrieds. It appears that the perception of commitment may make a difference to others.

Research indicates that about half of never-marrieds say they would like to marry eventually. Additionally, about a third of never-marrieds say that they are not sure if they ever want to marry. Whether they do or don't is an individual matter.

Often there is less expectation of monogamy among never-married couples — and generally, fewer expectations altogether.

As a general statement, never-marrieds may have a greater sense of having personal options than married couples. And in fact, there are fewer ties to bind non-married people together than their married counterparts. Sometimes individuals don't expect marriage would work, and so they choose to maintain their single status.

Life events for never-marrieds also can be more disruptive to the relationship. One example is job changes, specifically relocation. It is easier to move without the legal ties of marriage.

Another issue is pregnancy. We have observed that surprise pregnancies in high-conflict relationships seem more associated with non-married couples. Such stressors are more difficult to handle in non-married circumstances — with fewer ties that bind — than in married circumstances.

We have also generally observed lower levels of developed relationship expectations and relationship trust in non-married couples than married couples. That can mean more intense post-relationship discord for marrieds than for never-marrieds dissolving their relationships. Married couples often function with more expectations than never-marrieds, and this continues with post-relationship expectations. As a generalization, non-married couples may attach less firmly to each other than the marrieds. It is unclear if looser attachment leads to less trust, or the other way around.

The dynamics and effects for never-married parents (and their children) even when they stay together are similar, and the outcome upon dissolution of the parental relationship — single parenthood — is the same.

The risk of a never-married relationship is that it can be briefer than if married. The breakup rate is higher. Sometimes children in these relationships have more social and academic problems than children of marrieds.

TAKEAWAYS

While parents in a non-married relationship may not be constrained by legal ties, they face the same challenges as married couples when it comes to custody and parenting time.

Notes

Notes

_____

_____

_____

_____

_____

_____

_____

_____

_____

_____

_____

_____

_____

_____

_____

_____

_____

_____

_____

_____

_____

_____

_____

_____

_____

_____

CHAPTER 13

BLENDED FAMILIES

Family structures today are much more diverse, especially if you go back and compare to the 1960s. Nuclear families with two first-time married parents were historically the most prevalent — 73 percent of all families post-World War II and 61 percent as recently as 1980. The current figure is under 50 percent.

Since the 1960s, society has seen a proliferation of various types of non-nuclear family structures. There are single-parent families in which the child(ren) live with one parent and may or may not have contact with the other parent. Extended families involve a child(ren) living with one parent, but with other relatives of their parent. Grandparent families involve the child living with one or both grandparents, typically without either biological parent. Blended families are increasingly common and can include a child living with their parent — married or unmarried — and the parent's partner and/or the partner's children.

So many arrangements make for many challenges. Yet, the most important aspects for a family in any structure to function well are strong relationships that offer support, caring, and consistency.

THE CHALLENGES

A blended family or stepfamily consists of a couple — married or unmarried — and their collective children (those from the current relationship along with any from previous relationships).

Blended families are more common now than in the past. About one-third of marriages in the U.S. form a blended family, though many choose to cohabit rather than marry. In fact, in the United States, a majority of families are divorced. Also, the divorce rate for second marriages is higher — 60 percent — than for first marriages.

Blended families often originate rapidly and lack a shared past at their point of formation. That means it is typical that the child or children of one or both parents wouldn't have a history with the other parent or stepsiblings, though they may have a very regular and predictable relationship with their own parent. When the new parent figure is introduced, the child must adjust, just as the second parent figure also must adjust to the child or children.

Parents in such a relationship often assume their love for each other will automatically transfer to the children now involved. The adjustment often is not automatic and requires time, nurturance, and patience.

Even biological families typically evolve slowly with time. Parents often start out with a stable relationship before any children. Blended families, especially involving non-married partners, are formed much more readily. Relationships are more fluid and in the process of development.

Also, children may still crave a reunited nuclear family at the point of formation of the blended family. Having no say in the circumstances, they may still hope for a reunited nuclear family. Complicating the situation usually is that parents in the new blended family have less time, attention, and energy, even as new children are introduced. A child in such a circumstance may feel a loss of closeness to the biological parent. Not surprisingly, children also often feel a loss of position in the family under that circumstance.

Children often still are grieving the loss of their former family. Even if life in that household was difficult, the relationships there were at least predictable. The newly blended family is uncharted territory.

EFFECTIVE STEP-PARENTING

Effective step-parenting for both males and females involves recognition of the needs of children for guidance and to be heard. The building of trust with the stepchildren should be fostered. The supportive role to a child's biological mother or father should be emphasized and directives to the stepchild should be limited.

Reasonable stepparent expectations are important. It is also very important that disciplinary procedures are made clear by the new partner duo: Which parent figure is responsible for what aspects of discipline and rule-making?

Effective parenting by stepmothers involves a focus on non-judgment and understanding. Assertiveness can be helpful, especially if the child is angry or rejecting the stepmother.

While effective parenting by stepfathers often involves gradually assuming parental authority and discipline, it often works best if the biological parent remains primary in discipline and problem management.

Stepfathers typically experience less pressure and intensity directed at them. And the reality of the new stepfather can be interpreted differently by female and male children. Girls often focus on competition for the attention of their mother, while boys may begin with a rivalrous attitude toward the new male stepparent. That resentment can turn to appreciation of the same-sex adult in the household, depending on how the stepparent handles conflicts in the newly formed blended family.

A big focus should be put on the equality of relationship between the stepparent's own child or children (if any) and the stepchild.

Stepchildren should also be encouraged to voice their opinions, and should know their thoughts are valued by both the parent and the stepparent in the new family. Children need time and space to accept the new stepparent and the new family structure. The reality of occasional negative feelings such as loss, abandonment, and anger should be acknowledged. Mutual respect should be fostered.

This transition of roles in a newly blended family may take time — even two or three years. It requires trial and error, patience, caring, and a focus on understanding.

DEALING WITH TEENS

Adolescent children, as a subgroup of children, often feel at odds with the newly blended family. Adolescents typically are in the process of developing independence and autonomy. The needs of a new blended family require the opposite: greater closeness to begin to work together as a family. As the stepparent attempts to bond, the adolescent is trying to break free. Adolescents do best in an environment of low family conflict, which is not necessarily the case for a newly blended family.

Whether or not their parent figure is married to the new stepparent, children often consider and refer to the new parent figure as a stepparent, as will be referred to here. The stereotype of the stepmother as cold, demanding, rivalrous, and prepared to dislike her stepchildren is occasionally true, but often not. Frankly, it can be a complex relationship on both sides. Stepmothers can encounter fierce loyalties by stepchildren for their mother, who no longer lives with them as before.

The age of the child in a newly blended family can be a factor in how the circumstances play out. Rivalry issues are less frequent with young children than with teens. Also, adolescent girls are at the greatest risk of viewing a new stepfather as an intruder, and of having issues relating to loyalty to the biological mother. Sometimes in those circumstances the stepfather — and in other cases, the child — may withdraw and become a polite stranger as he feels pushed out of the family system from the standpoint of the adolescent girl.

TAKEAWAYS

Blended family adjustments often take time. Effective parenting may be somewhat different for stepmothers and stepfathers. Becoming part of a blended family is a big adjustment for everyone. Adults need to remember that it's a time of huge transition. Children's opinions and feelings should be heard and acknowledged.

Notes

Notes

CHAPTER 14

SAME-SEX ISSUES

The landmark United States Supreme Court decision of Obergefell v. Hodges in June, 2015 brought marriage equality to all 50 states. This decision established the rights of same-sex couples to marry. It requires every state to recognize same-sex marriages performed in other states and other countries. It also gives same-sex couples the legal right to marry anywhere in the United States.

As this book is being produced only five years later, same-sex couples still face challenges and problems when their relationships dissolve and families come apart.

EQUITABLE PARENT DOCTRINE

In Michigan and many other states, a concept known as the equitable parent doctrine allows a third party who is not a biological parent to exercise parental rights, including parenting time with the child, as well as be able to legally seek custody. The problem is that in Michigan, for example, the Court of Appeals has ruled against a lesbian nonbiological mother; the court has limited the equitable parent doctrine to married couples.

This ruling and similar ones in other states mean that any same-sex couple who could not marry before the U.S. Supreme Court decision allowing same-sex marriage will not have the same rights regarding custody and parenting time if they are not married. Unmarried heterosexual couples have full rights regarding custody, but these rights still do not apply to unmarried same-sex couples.

In another situation where a marriage was formalized in Canada, a Michigan court after a lengthy battle ruled that if an established custodial environment can be proven, the nonbiological parent has legal standing to file an action seeking equitable parenthood. (Note: "Standing" means the right of a person to file a court action to seek legal relief.)

The key in Michigan and other states is that to legally seek relief over parenting time and custodial issues, there must be a valid marriage; otherwise, the nonbiological parent is not viewed as equal to heterosexual couples by the courts. At this point, their rights are limited. This is an area that many think needs to change so that all parents, whether married or not, can have court jurisdiction to pursue rights for custody and parenting time with their children, even if they are not the biological parent.

BIRTH CERTIFICATES

Another important issue facing same-sex couples relates to birth certificates. The key is whether same-sex couple parents can have both parents' names listed on the child's birth certificate in situations where the child is born to or adopted by the couple.

Before the Supreme Court decision, there was no "marital presumption" that children born during a same-sex, non-marital relationship were children of that relationship. If one parent were the birth parent, that parent would be listed on the birth certificate. If the other parent or parent figure in a relationship was not the biological father or the birth mother, he or she would not be listed.

Since the Obergefell Supreme Court decision, same-sex married couples enjoy identical rights and privileges as heterosexual married couples. This means that all children born during a marriage, whether a same-sex or heterosexual marriage, are presumed to be children of that marriage, and both married parents should be listed on the birth certificate.

There were situations where parents in same-sex relationships or marriages before the Supreme Court ruling were unable to list both parents on their child's birth certificate. They may now go to county clerk offices where a birth certificate is registered to modify or correct birth certificates to reflect both parents on these important documents.

It is important to remember that a birth certificate is an administrative document that records the fact of a birth of a child and who the parents are. It is not a custody order and does not have the same important impact that a court order regarding custody or parenting time has on the life of a family or the rights and responsibilities that parents have with regard to each other and their children.

The issues over names on birth certificates where babies are born through artificial insemination to same-sex couples who are not married and in situations where both parties are infertile are being hotly contested as this book is being written.

While it is important to correct and update birth certificates to reflect legally recognized parents as a result of the changes in the laws, the current state of the law is that birth certificates cannot be amended to add a parent to a birth certificate absent genetic contribution, adoption, or gestational primacy. It should be noted that a birth certificate neither constitutes a legal filing of parentage nor does it independently convey or terminate parental rights.

There are cases involving the rights to move out of state where there is an equitable parent, as well as all of the issues that couples face with children when there are same-sex issues that make matters more complicated.

In fact, this is a very complicated area. If you are a member of a same-sex couple or are facing any of these issues, it is critical that you consult with an attorney who handles these types of situations.

THE PSYCHOLOGICAL PARENT DOCTRINE

So what happens if a same-sex couple has raised children without benefit or the legal rights of marriage, and then they break up? If one is not a legally recognized parent, either by lack of marriage or biological connection with the child, then other legal principles or theories may apply to address and protect the parent-child relationships.

Eleven states currently recognize a concept known as the psychological parent doctrine or something similar. Recognized by many courts, it generally means that if a parent has been involved in every aspect of a child's life, even if he or she is not a biological parent, certain legal rights may apply after the end of a marriage or relationship.

A psychological parent is one who, on a day-to-day basis, through interaction, companionship, interplay, and mutuality fulfills the psychological needs of the child. This adult becomes an essential focus of the child's life, for the parent is not only the source of fulfillment of a child's physical needs, but also the source of emotional and psychological support.

The wanted child is the one who is loved, valued, appreciated, and viewed as an essential person by the adult who cares for that child. This relationship may exist between a child and an adult; it also depends on the category into which the adult falls — biological, adoptive, foster, or common law — and on the quality and mutuality of the interaction. (This is language from an Alaska court case.)

The psychological parent doctrine focuses on the child and his or her psychological bond with an adult, and the effects on the child if that bond is suddenly severed. This doctrine puts the focus on the best interests of the child, not on the legal relationships between the respective parental figures and the child.

As the definition of "family" evolves with same-sex marriage and recent changes in the law and recognition of these families, the courts — and society — are struggling to catch up. The key is that the legal system should consider what is in the best interests of children whose parents appear in court.

It is common sense that it is in the best interests of the child to have as much love and affection from an adult figure, regardless of legal or biological status. The trend should be to encourage relationships between the child and both parental figures.

Dignity, respect, open-mindedness, and a willingness to recognize all types of families will assist the courts in navigating this new territory. Only then will a sense of equal justice for all prevail.

TAKEAWAYS

Five years ago, same-sex marriages became legal throughout the United States, but there remain some unresolved issues for same-sex couples when it comes to child custody. Regardless, the focus must be on the best interests of a child and not preconceived or out-of-date legal notions and laws.

The authors thank Richard Roane, Esq., for contributing to this chapter.

Notes

Notes

CHAPTER 15

WHAT ABOUT GRANDPARENTS?

An important issue in the convoluted world of child custody and parenting time is whether grandparents have any legally supported rights to see their grandchildren. This is an area that has been fraught with litigation and controversy over the years.

Grandparents can provide a loving relationship with their grandchildren. In many cases, they are a source of stability and continuity for children — and support for parents going through a separation and divorce.

We have been involved in cases involving grandparents having time with their grandchildren. In some situations, it has been possible to obtain grandparent visitation; in others, the courts have ruled that under the circumstances, the grandparents had no rights to see their grandchildren at all.

LEGAL ISSUES

In 2000, after many years of litigation and uncertainty, the U.S. Supreme Court, in the case of Troxel v. Granville, ruled that a Washington State statute was invalid when it permitted "any person" to petition for visitation rights at "any time." The ruling authorized state courts to grant such rights whenever visitation served the child's best interests. The key here is not what the grandparents want, but whether such access is in the grandchildren's best interests.

This issue has been dealt with throughout the United States. In Michigan, the law is now that there is a presumption that a fit parent's decision to deny grandparenting time does not create a substantial risk of harm to the child's mental, physical, or emotional heath. In fact, under the laws in Michigan, the court may also dismiss the action if two fit parents sign an affidavit stating that they both oppose an order for grandparenting time.

This collectively means that grandparents have an uphill battle to obtain time with their grandchildren when the parents oppose it. The key is the Supreme Court case that lays out very limited rights for grandparents.

Grandparents seeking time with their grandchildren have to show why it is not only beneficial to the grandchildren, but also why denying the visitation creates a substantial risk of harm to the child's mental, physical, or emotional health. Based upon current law, this is an uphill battle for most grandparents. Every case is different and it is critical for any grandparent to consult with an attorney before deciding whether to proceed with a legal petition. In order to prevail, the scale of justice must be tipped in a client's favor slightly — perhaps by an extra 5 or 10 percent over a 50-50 balance.

Besides showing why visitation is best for the grandchild, grandparents must overcome arguments presented by a parent who is opposing their request for visitation. If a grandparent has been involved in a close and loving relationship and has spent a tremendous amount of time with the grandchildren, that can work in the grandparent's favor.

Grandparents in Michigan have argued that they have a fundamental right to a relationship with their grandchildren. This argument has been rejected by the appellate courts in Michigan.

WHAT THE LAW SAYS

The applicable law in Michigan states that a grandparent may seek grandparenting time if:

(a) An action for divorce, separate maintenance, or annulment involving the child's parents is pending before the court;

(b) The child's parents are divorced, separated under a judgment of separate maintenance, or have had their marriage annulled;

(c) The child's parent, who is a child of the grandparents, is deceased;

(d) The child's parents have never been married, they are not residing in the same household and paternity has been established;

(e) Legal custody of the child has been given to a person other than the child's parent or the child is placed outside of and does not reside in the home of a parent; or

(f) In the year preceding the commencement of the action for grandparenting time, the grandparent provided an established custodial environment for the child, whether or not the grandparent had custody under a court order.

CASE-BY-CASE

These are complicated issues that must be reviewed on a case-by-case basis. We have had courts grant grandparent visitation where the grandparents have had a long-term and close relationship with a grandchild and where a parent without some good reason is trying to terminate the relationship. The key is that there has been a close and long-term relationship and there is not a good reason to change that. This is where there has been a divorce or the death of a parent.

On the other hand, we have had cases where clients have lost their son through death and the former daughter-in-law has cut off all contact with the grandchildren. The courts have ruled in favor of the parent against the grandparent. In some of these cases, grandparents have lost any contact with their grandchildren.

Our advice to grandparents who are put in this sad and often tragic situation is to make sure that they talk to an attorney who specializes in family law and is familiar with issues involving the laws of the state where the grandparent visitation is to occur.

In addition, it is important to try to maintain a good relationship with children and daughters- and sons-in-law so that in the event of a divorce or death, it is still possible to maintain a relationship with the grandchildren.

There is a saying that it takes a village to raise a child. As grandparents, we believe that children need frequent contact with loving grandparents as well as other family members.

TAKEAWAYS

Grandparents have some rights when it comes to getting visitation time with their grandchildren. Sadly, the laws make this an uphill battle, with the rights of parents tending to take precedence over those of grandparents, regardless of what may be in the children's best interests. Typically children in situations of dissolved families benefit from relationships with their extended families.

Notes

_____

_____

_____

_____

_____

_____

_____

_____

_____

_____

_____

_____

_____

_____

_____

_____

_____

_____

_____

_____

_____

_____

_____

_____

CHAPTER 16

OVER THE STATE LINE

O

ne of the most difficult circumstances of child custody conflicts involves one parent moving out of state after a custody agreement has been reached or even during a divorce or custody dispute. Often it is difficult or impossible to create a shared custodial arrangement, especially if the parents have been sharing about equal time with the children.

Michigan has two rules. One is called the 100-Mile Rule which prohibits a move of more than 100 miles if a parent wants to relocate with the children. Prior to that change in the law, a parent could move from metropolitan Detroit in southeast Michigan to the northern part of the state without court permission because the move was within the state, though it may have meant a distance of hundreds of miles.

On the other hand, if a parent wanted to move from Detroit to Toledo, Ohio (about 60 miles away), court permission was required. Michigan and many states require court permission after a custody order has been entered before a parent can move out of state with minor children. This is true if a move is contemplated during a divorce or custody proceeding as well.

WHAT THE COURT LOOKS FOR

When there is a long-distance move, the parenting plan should be adjusted to accommodate the move and distance between the parents. Some of the key factors many states consider include:
- The custodial parent's reasons for wanting to relocate with the children.
- The time spent with the other parent now and after the proposed relocation.
- The effect of the move upon the children's physical, educational, and emotional development.

- The effect upon the non-custodial or shared custodial parent's parenting time/visitation rights.
- Whether the relocation will enhance the general quality of life for both the parent seeking the relocation and the child.
- The move should be prompted by a legitimate reason — not to deprive the other parent of parenting time. It also should not be in retaliation for a bitter divorce or custody battle.

We are using the laws in Michigan as examples, and advise consulting an attorney in your state if you are considering a move out of state with your children. The laws differ from state to state, as do the practices regarding changes of domicile.

In deciding these complicated issues, courts will look at the following factors:
- The prospective advantages of the move in terms of its likely capacity for improving the general quality of life for the custodial parent and the children.
- The integrity of the motives of the custodial parent in seeking the move.

The court will want to determine whether the removal is inspired primarily by the desire to defeat or frustrate visitation by the non-custodial parent, and whether the custodial parent is likely to comply with substitute visitation orders when she or he is no longer subject to the jurisdiction of the courts in the previous state.
- The integrity of the non-custodial parent's motives in resisting the removal and consideration of the extent to which, if at all, the opposition is intended to secure a financial advantage in respect to continuing support obligations.
- Finally, the court must be satisfied that there will be a realistic opportunity for visitation in lieu of the original pattern established. The new plan should provide an adequate basis for preserving and fostering the parental relationship with the non-custodial parent if removal is allowed.

A DIFFICULT DECISION

Change of domicile is one of the most difficult issues a family court judge must consider. Oakland County Family Court Judge Mary Ellen Brennan was a recent guest on *Practical Law* (Co-author Attorney Henry S. Gornbein's television show). Currently the Chief Judge of the family court in the county, she is an excellent jurist who cares about the people who come in front of her and often agonizes over decisions like granting permission for a long-distance move with children after divorce.

She has been a judge since 2008 and has spent that entire time on the Oakland County Family Court. Her docket includes divorce, child custody, paternity, juvenile delinquency, neglect, and abuse.

Asked about moves out of state of more than 100 miles, Judge Brennan said, "That can be really challenging. A lot of people reach agreements on their own, whether married or not, and are successful at co-parenting and can work it out where there is a move.

"The problem is when the parties cannot work out these issues on their own. The key is that the kids will be moved from the environment where they were when the relationship ended.

"In Michigan prior to 2008 before the economy crashed, it was very difficult to obtain a move out of state. After Michigan was crippled and there were no jobs, moves were more easily granted. Now the economy is good again in Michigan and nationwide.

"It is tough to obtain a change of domicile now. You have to convince the judge that this move will benefit to the extent that it overrides the other parent's desires to oppose it."

Judge Brennan doesn't only consider the economic motivation for such a move. She also wants to know about the schools in the new environment; what types of family support there will be; and what life will look like in Florida, for example, versus the life the family led in Michigan.

What about the impact of remarriage to someone from another state?

She says, "Remarriage is a consideration, but not the only one. Those are tough when a woman is remarrying. The focus has to be on the child. Just removing the life of the new spouse who has a better job is not enough. The economic increase and standard of living is just one of the factors and is not enough by itself."

Judge Brennan has to be comfortable for the move to be granted.

In most cases, parents have joint legal custody with shared parenting time. Shared custody is the norm now versus 20 or 30 years ago when one parent would have primary physical custody and most of the time with the children.

In considering requests to move far away, Judge Brennan looks at the judgment of divorce, paternity, or custody that is in place. If it is sole legal custody, she goes in one direction. If it is joint legal custody, she has to look at the environment both of the parents provide, and there will also be a higher standard of proof for the parent initiating the move.

In addition, she pulls the curtain back to see what the reality is. If the parties have not followed the order and the father has spent a lot more time than the order stated, this can be significant. Appellate courts want the judges to look behind the scenes.

Judge Brennan also wants to know if there's a parenting time plan that can be put in place that is equivalent to the one in Michigan. And how do you fashion a parenting time schedule that is equal or apportioned 60-40 in Florida versus if everyone lives here in Michigan? You probably can't.

Skype and FaceTime can be used for communication, though Judge Brennan doesn't believe that's the same as a hug or physical personal contact. Sending the children to the other parent for the summer is not the same, either. A young teen who is in school all year and then comes to Michigan for the summer cannot see her friends or get a job. It is difficult.

The easiest cases are those where one parent is not involved and has very little economic or emotional involvement. If the order says sole legal custody and the actuality is sole legal custody with one parent doing all of the daily decisions, all that is required in those cases is the court's permission. Basically the court just has to have a brief hearing and grant permission. One judge has said it is like telling the parent to stand in the driveway and wave goodbye. The hands-on, 24/7 parent has a significant advantage. The hard ones are when both parents are hands-on.

Judge Brennan also tries to view the request through the eyes of the child. That is what the statute requires. It is a case-by-case situation. Every situation is different.

In one situation, a child had an interest in diving. There was a coach in California and the child was home schooled and wanted to pursue her career in diving with dreams of becoming an Olympic diver. She was age 13 and overall seemed responsible enough for the court to consider her wishes. Mom wanted the move and Dad opposed it. In this case, what the child wanted was critical. Judge Brennan granted the move.

In another example, a father and sole provider lost his job in Michigan through no fault of his own and couldn't find a replacement here despite doing everything he could think of to get one. He had, however, found one in Kentucky and it was waiting for him. Judge Brennan felt he'd tried to find similar employment in Michigan and when that proved to be impossible, it was reason to justify a move.

Motivation is another factor the judge considers. Is the move prompted by a desire to avoid paying child support, or to attempt to cut the child off from the other parent?

She also takes family ties into consideration. What if there is a job change to Michigan from another state and all family ties are in that other state? Judge Brennan feels that family ties are important if the relationships have continued over the years and are healthy and close with travel back and forth.

Regarding issues of parental alienation and domestic violence, Judge Brennan stated: "If there is domestic violence between the parties, whether or not it is witnessed by or in front of the child, it is a factor to be considered. If a husband or wife or an unmarried parent is trying to remove himself or herself from a situation with domestic violence — if there is an attempt to move with family support and financial support, these can be strong issues favoring granting a move."

And what happens when children don't want to spend the entire summer in or out of state? In this situation, the judge has an excellent family counselor step in. The counselor will try to look at specifics including drive time and what makes sense in a particular case. For example, if there is a move from Michigan to Kentucky, the court will be creative and look at what can be done to provide as much time as possible in Michigan and Kentucky and also to deal with the economics in order to hammer out a parenting time schedule that is as realistic and even as possible.

Airline schedules and finances are issues. Judge Brennan places the financial burden on the parent who moves unless the parent who is left behind is making a far greater income.

And what if the parties cannot resolve their case and the judge has to rule? That's when the best interests factors come front and center again. The judge talks to the child or children to see how much time the child will want to spend in Michigan and in the other state. The older the child, the more the child's desires become important.

Judge Brennan gave an example of a case in which she granted a move for a child who had asthma and could benefit from the climate in Arizona, where the parent wanted to move.

In the end, the judge prefers for parents to work it out on their own, saying, "You know your kids and family situation best. You know what will work for your family best. If there is any way that you can make the decision on your own, that is best. This is what the judge will say from the bench before she has to make a decision."

TAKEAWAYS

Change of domicile and the relocation of your children is one of the most difficult areas of family law. When one parent is trying to take the child to another state, it immediately changes the custodial and parenting time arrangement. Most situations are no-win. This is an area that you should carefully discuss with your attorney and/or your psychotherapist before you make a decision. Every case is fact-specific, and the laws differ from state to state.

Notes

CHAPTER 17

BEYOND BORDERS

News stories often feature situations where children have gone on vacation with one parent and are not returned. This is not only dramatic, but it also represents a very complicated area of the law. We have dealt with international child custody disputes, including cases between the United States and the United Kingdom, Mexico, Italy, and Israel, though it happens all over the world. If you are in this situation or concerned about potentially facing such circumstances, it is essential to talk to an attorney who is an expert in such cases. Often these scenarios can develop into criminal cases because kidnapping can be involved.

Recently there was a well-publicized case between the United States and Brazil where the children were lost to their father for many years and were only returned after the mother had passed away. The mother was a citizen of Brazil and the Brazilian authorities never cooperated.

FEDERAL LAW APPLIES

In the United States, the federal Parental Kidnapping Prevention Act facilitates the prosecution of parents who kidnap their children. The law calls for states to give full faith and credit to child custody determinations made by other states, provided that certain conditions are met. It also provides for a Federal Parental Locator Service (FPLS) to find parents or children in determining or enforcing custody in parental kidnapping cases.

The FPLS is a national location system operated by the Federal Office of Child Support Enforcement to assist states in locating non-custodial parents, putative fathers, and custodial parties for the establishment of paternity and child support obligations, as well as for the enforcement and modification of orders for child support, custody, and visitation.

For international cases, the Hague Convention on the Civil Aspects of International Child Abduction is the prevailing law. The goal of the Hague Convention, ratified by the United States in 1986, is to curb international abductions of children by providing judicial remedies to those seeking the return of a child who has been wrongfully taken.

Eighty-two member nations participate in the Hague Convention. However, many countries in Africa, Asia, and the Middle East are not parties to the Hague Convention. Also, sometimes because of other complexities, countries that are members of the Hague Convention make it difficult for the return of the child who has allegedly been kidnapped by a parent. Often, foreign police and government agencies become involved. The situation can rapidly get out of hand.

The key is to be careful if you are in a relationship that has international implications, whether married or not, if a child or children are involved. If you foresee possible difficulties, consult with an attorney at once. It could be very important to explore ways to prevent your child from being removed from the state where you are residing as well as from the United States. Sometimes one parent will move with the child to another state and then the legal battles commence. Here, careful planning and sound legal advice can be critical. Sometimes a passport of a child is held in escrow to prevent absconding.

TRAVELING WITH CHILDREN

Now, if you are traveling abroad with your children, there are some issues to consider. If a minor is under the age of 14, a parent wishing to obtain a passport must establish proof of citizenship and proof of relationship. Both parents must appear together to apply for the passport, or one parent must appear and submit the other parent's notarized statement of consent authorizing issuance of a passport for the child along with primary evidence of sole authority to apply.

It is critical when traveling with a child, whether in the United States or abroad, to carry written consent from the other parent. We also strongly recommend that a medical authorization be carried in the event of a medical problem or emergency so no issues can be raised, and so necessary treatment can promptly take place.

TAKEAWAYS

Interstate and international child custody disputes and kidnapping can be extremely complex, difficult, and even treacherous. Talking to an experienced attorney with expertise in this specialized area of the law is critical. Promptly consulting with legal authorities when necessary can avoid a potential nightmare.

Notes

Notes

CHAPTER 18

DOCUMENT EVERYTHING

Keeping a journal if you are involved in a child custody or parenting time dispute can be critical. Maintaining a calendar is also very important.

A journal is a record of daily events that relate to the best interests of your child. It is a who, what, when, and where description. A calendar is used to keep track of schedules and can be posted in a common area so that everyone knows what is going on regarding daily routines.

WHY JOURNAL?

There are several reasons for keeping a journal:

1. It helps prepare your case as you proceed toward a hearing or trial.
2. It helps prepare your strongest case for negotiations, mediation, and possible settlement.
3. By keeping a journal, you will be documenting important issues and will not have to be emailing or calling your attorney or psychotherapist after each incident. This helps to save attorney fees and also is a way to strengthen your case.
4. You and your attorney and/or psychotherapist will be able to discuss key issues and incidents at one time and you will have all of this information at your fingertips.
5. Keeping this journal can also help reduce your stress. By writing about incidents and issues, you can effectively manage issues in a constructive and therapeutic manner.
6. In a child custody case, your journal is important to keep track of any incidents involving your child or children. It is also an important way to position yourself for a hearing or trial consistent with the best interests of your child.
7. Examples in your journal should include a daily log of what you are doing with your child or children. It should include information regarding appointments, such as doctors and dentists and who transported the kids. It should note any problems during the day. For example, were words exchanged between you and the other parent? Was there a confrontation or argument over a child-related issue? This should be written down. You should also keep a log as to what you do each day with the children and what the other parent does. This is a way to really keep track of what is going on in the life of your child on a daily basis.

If there is a child custody evaluation as part of your case, your journal can be very helpful in informing the psychologist regarding key points.

OTHER ISSUES

If there are school- or health-related issues, these should be part of the journal, too. If a child is sick or having an emotional issue, it should be documented. Any disciplinary problems should be in the journal. The key is who, what, where, and when.

You will have reviewed the child custody laws in your state as you work with your attorney and your journal should also reflect what is in the best interests of your child as you move forward. It should be structured in a fashion to try to track issues consistent with your child's best interests on a daily basis. The journal does not have to go into great detail, but should provide an outline to build on as your case moves forward.

If your case lasts for six months or more, this journal will be additionally important, as it will provide a timeline of key developments since you started your case to the point of any hearing, mediation, trial, or settlement.

Keep your journal in a safe place. Make sure that no one else can see it but your attorney. You do not want your spouse or partner who is the other parent having a copy of this journal or knowing about it. If you keep it online, make sure that it is protected from being hacked. Retain both digital and printed copies. Preferably keep one copy in a safe place outside of the house.

MAINTAINING A CALENDAR

Whether or not you and the other parent are living together during this period, it is important to have a calendar so that all events are recorded. These should include the dates and times for medical and dental or counseling appointments for your child or children. The calendar should also note school days and events, all extracurricular activities such as sporting events and practices, and any special events in your child's or children's lives.

The calendar should not be used as a weapon, but as a tool to make sure that your child's life is running as smoothly as possible, even if you and the other parent are now functioning as separate entities. The calendar should also include the days that each of you has your child and what the full parenting time schedule is. The last thing that you want to do is be in a battle over whose day it is and/or a pickup or delivery time regarding a practice, game, or other event.

In any shared parenting time arrangement, it is critical that you put your child's interests ahead of any strife and try to make sure that the transitions, pickups, and drop-offs are handled as smoothly as possible. You do not want your child waiting after school or at day care or a special event with no one there to pick him or her up. Don't hurt your child!

TAKEAWAYS

Keeping a journal and a calendar are critical documents as you prepare a case regarding the custody and parenting time of your child. These documents will help you to keep track of events and details as you go through a custody or parenting time dispute. Be brief and specific: stick to who, what, where, and when. Your journal, along with a calendar, are important building blocks to use as you prepare with your attorney and psychotherapist for settlement, mediation, or trial.

Notes

CHAPTER 19

CHOOSING A PSYCHOTHERAPIST

The stress of court-related conflict often can trigger feelings of pessimism, hopelessness, sadness, uncertainty, anger, tension, and worry. Stress also can trigger problematic behaviors such as increased or excessive use of drugs or alcohol.

Sometimes people can become argumentative, constantly annoyed, oppositional, or aggressive. Some become tearful and withdrawn. Children can also become reactive to their home environment. They may act out in similar ways, which reflects that they are experiencing similar feelings.

Often it is wise to respond to problems rather than continuing to just wait for them to improve or go away. The development of problematic feelings and behaviors in custody-related domestic situations is not uncommon because of the intensity of the circumstances.

SELECTING A PROFESSIONAL

One productive response can be to seek professional assistance from a licensed mental health professional. Such assistance can take the path of consultation or psychotherapy.

A licensed mental health professional with expertise in human behavior assessment, diagnosis, and treatment can often prove to be a source of helpful support and guidance. Psychotherapists work with their clients to adjust their thoughts, feelings, and attitudes to develop healthier, more effective patterns of behavior. This just might be what you need.

Professionals from many fields have begun to do psychotherapy. Licensed psychologists, social workers, and psychiatrists often have the most extensive training and experience. Others in recent years who have done psychotherapy are licensed professional counselors, nurse practitioners, and marriage and family therapists. Capable people exist in all of these professions.

The professional you select should be specific to you, your situation, and your needs. First, look for someone with experience in family conflict and individual problems. Someone who has specialized in divorce and related issues is best.

Some think the gender of the psychotherapist is important. Most professionals likely would not agree, though it is important that you feel comfortable. If you absolutely do not want a psychotherapist of a certain gender, then such a selection probably should be avoided, since you want to focus on identifying and improving your issues rather than being sidetracked.

Try to find recommendations from people you know and trust who have had experience with psychotherapy that is at least somewhat related to your circumstances. Online resources can be checked, though ratings themselves may not be helpful. Checking out an online site that requires credentialing such as the *Psychology Today* Therapist Directory can be helpful, and may be a good place to start. Request recommendations from your family physician or seek out known mental health professionals in your area. Court personnel are also often aware of experienced psychotherapists for your situation.

TREATMENT APPROACHES

Psychotherapists may be trained in various models of treatment. As a general statement, our experience is that in family-related contexts such as domestic relations/custody issues, cognitions are important to consider and so are emotions. In our opinion, usually in such situations a psychodynamic approach involving a focus on unconscious motivations may be less immediately productive than understanding how your family system has worked and how your new arrangement functions.

Verifying licensing credentials can be important to ensure that you receive quality professional treatment. Licensure laws exist to protect the public by restricting practice to those qualified to practice. Check your state's licensing website to verify the potential psychotherapist's credentials. Licensing boards also follow strict codes of ethics. Renewal of licensure often depends on demonstrated continued education and competency.

Verifying training also can be important. For example, doctoral level psychologists typically spend five, six, or seven years in education and training after graduation from college with a bachelor's degree. Some psychologists even receive training following their final degree.

What characteristics should you look for in a psychotherapist? A prime quality of an effective psychotherapist is their being a good listener. You may get an initial impression from your first contact, which often is talking on the phone. But the more important impression is gained from the face-to-face contact of the first appointment.

Another important characteristic is flexibility. Is the psychotherapist receptive to receiving and answering your questions? Ask questions about their professional experiences and determine if this psychotherapist is experienced in areas related to your issues.

Assess how focused the psychotherapist is on you. Your psychotherapist should seem to be compassionate and nonjudgmental. The psychotherapist should not be talking about his/her experiences but rather should be asking you questions. If instead you are hearing much about the psychotherapist's own marriage, family, children, or special interests, it might be a sign that this particular psychotherapist will not be a good choice.

The degree of success in psychotherapy has much to do with the degree of rapport and alliance a client establishes with the psychotherapist, who should only be focused on the needs of the client. The relationship is very important.

Over time, the client should begin to feel more capable and in control. An increased sense of resilience also is important. Psychotherapy should help you feel more goal-oriented and also should help you establish and meet goals.

TAKEAWAYS

Court-related conflict in divorce and custody matters can wreak havoc and create stress and behavioral issues in both adults and children. Seeing a psychotherapist who is a good fit can help limit the chaos, and help those affected by divorce feel more secure and in control.

Notes

CHAPTER 20

TRIAL TIPS: PREPARING A CUSTODY CASE

Throughout the chapters of this book, we have emphasized the fact that trial should be a last resort. Any family court judge will tell you that the best decisions are those made by the parents — not by a stranger in a black robe.

When you go through a trial, you will rarely like the result. Less than 1 percent of all family law cases ever go to trial. If you are in that 1 percent, what can you expect? While your judge will do his or her best under the circumstances, it's the judge who is in control if you go to trial — not you and not the other parent. The judge will have a bird's-eye evaluative and judgmental view of your life and the lives of your children.

The decision of the court will be based upon a limited amount of time, select information, and strict rules of evidence. We have spoken to many people who have gone through a trial and many who have in some sense prevailed. Not one feels they "won" anything. There, in fact, is nothing to "win" in a custody trial.

The trial process in a custody matter is highly adversarial and very stressful. Trials dredge up imperfections in you and your spouse, and probably also in your children. The process often "burns bridges."

WHAT HAPPENS AT TRIAL?

Preparation for a trial is critical. There is an old saying that attorneys should never ask a question to which they do not already know the answer. Trials rarely go the way the participants think, and they do have surprises, but rarely is there a slam-dunk or gotcha moment. Some cases do have a smoking gun, but those are infrequent.

In a child custody or change of domicile case, the judge by law focuses on what is in the best interests of the child. That is true in almost every state. Sadly, that usually means you and your attorney will emphasize building you up while trying to tear the other parent down. Hurtful things that you say in open court are difficult to take back. After a trial, it will be much more difficult to fashion or rebuild a constructive relationship consistent with the best interests of your children.

One of the first steps is to determine who you will call to testify. Carefully review in advance who the potential witnesses are and their likely testimony.

Typically you and the other parent are key witnesses. There may be a psychologist involved if there has been a psychological evaluation. Relatives like grandparents, medical treaters, teachers, friends, or other professionals may be on the list.

We have observed and learned from experience that many judges have a low threshold for boredom. They have many, many cases and limited time for each one. If you call witnesses to testify, it is critical that you use only those whose testimony you consider essential. If there are witnesses to physical or verbal abuse or domestic violence, these can be critical. Keep in mind, you will be dredging up bad memories and then having these situations examined.

But a parade of family members telling about how good you are and how bad the other parent is typically is a waste of time. You do not want to waste the judge's time. If you have several character witnesses, don't call more than one or two.

Meet in the presence of your attorney with the witnesses you intend to call. Thorough preparation of all witnesses is critical for any trial.

If you have expert witnesses such as a psychologist, personal psychotherapist, or perhaps your medical doctor, a good attorney will make sure that their testimony has been discussed in advance. There may be a private investigator or local police officer as well.

Ask your lawyer if it would be helpful to obtain school records, report cards, medical reports and files, any psychological evaluations that have been done, police reports, or other evidence if there has been domestic violence. If there are issues regarding special education or special needs, it may be necessary to call a specialist in this area as well.

If substance abuse is involved, it may be important to have a driving record and prescription evidence in the event of a prescription drug problem.

Other types of evidence can involve photographs, emails, text messages, and cell phone and computer records. Your smartphone or computer can be your best friend or worst enemy, depending upon your behavior.

If there is a move or change of domicile at issue, then comparative records of schools, climate, jobs, and income can all be relevant. You and your attorney should be prepared for every possible contingency as you get ready for a custody trial or hearing.

Another issue to discuss in advance is who should be your first witness. Sometimes you may want to call your soon-to-be former spouse or the other parent as a hostile or adverse witness. These are all issues that should be carefully thought out.

The opening statement — whether delivered by you or your attorney — is key. This is when you tell the judge what you want regarding custody and parenting time with your children and why. It is important to be clear about what you hope to achieve, but do it concisely and clearly.

An attorney who rambles or is not able to get to the point quickly is not going to do well. This is also true of a parent who is seeking custody or a change of custody or domicile.

Finally comes the closing argument, which is presented by the attorneys or the litigants (if one or both litigants is representing themselves and where there are no attorneys) at the close of the actual proofs of the case. Here it is important to summarize, but to do it in a fashion that is brief and to the point. Again, it is important to emphasize the highlights of your case and the lowlights of the other side, but to do it quickly. It is a chance to highlight and summarize the reasons why you should prevail in court.

TAKEAWAYS

This chapter makes suggestions for trial preparation. It covers witnesses, preparation, exhibits, and basic advice. Every case is different. The key is to present what you want and why you want it. You must show why the relief you are seeking from the court is in the best interests of your child. To repeat, we emphasize that trial should be a last resort!

To see a list of Sample Questions for Trial, please see Appendix I.

Notes

CHAPTER 21

GUARDIANS AND PARENTING COORDINATORS

Courts often appoint a third party to assist in the resolution of custody and parenting time issues. In high-conflict cases, a court wants additional legal expertise and sometimes more mental health expertise — or both. This would involve the use of Guardians Ad Litem and Parenting Coordinators.

GUARDIAN AD LITEM

The court appoints a Guardian Ad Litem (GAL) to assist in determining the best interests of the child in a custody or parenting time dispute. The GAL is usually an attorney but sometimes can be a mental health professional.

A GAL becomes familiar with the parties and children in a custody or parenting time dispute, and also becomes somewhat familiar with the experience and views of professionals who work with the parties and children such as psychotherapists, pediatricians, teachers, and the like. A GAL assists the court by making recommendations to a judge about what is in the best interests of the child in a child custody or parenting time dispute. A GAL will work with the parties and their attorneys to resolve a case and avoid a contested trial or hearing.

We have been involved in some very high-conflict custody battles where the role of the GAL was invaluable in helping the parties stop battling and more functionally relate to each other in the best interests of the children. Some situations involved cases of alleged parental alienation. Some cases involved very young children and overnight parenting time. Some cases involved matters in which there were multiple contacts with Child Protective Services.

The costs of the GAL are often divided between the parties. In some situations where one of the parents and their attorneys may overutilize the GAL or act in bad faith, the fees for the GAL's services can be apportioned other than equally. In addition, where there is a large disparity in incomes, the fees of the GAL often are divided based upon the earnings of the parties.

In many instances, if the case cannot be resolved, the GAL will be requested to prepare a written report and recommendation to the judge. A GAL also can be called to testify as a witness in an effort to make a determination as to what is in the best interests of the child.

By spending focused time with the parties and the minor children, the GAL is able to obtain information useful to the court. Many judges will weigh the information and report of the GAL quite heavily in making a decision regarding custody or parenting time.

Laws and requirements differ from state to state. The Guardian Ad Litem's duties have been described as follows.

1. The obligations of the attorney-client privilege, when the GAL is a lawyer.
2. To serve as the independent representative for the child's best interests and be entitled to full and active participation in all aspects of litigation and access to all relevant information regarding the child.
3. To determine the facts of the case by conducting an independent investigation including but not limited to interviewing the child, social workers, family members, and others as necessary, and reviewing relevant reports and other information.
4. To meet with or observe the child and assess the child's needs and wishes with regard to the representation and the issues in the case.
5. The court may allow alternative means of contact with the child if good cause is shown on the record.
6. To explain to the child, taking into account the child's ability to understand the proceedings, the GAL's role. A mental health professional is trained for this role and can be critical with regard to this function.
7. To file all necessary pleadings and papers and independently call witnesses on the child's behalf.
8. To attend all hearings and substitute representation for the child only with court approval.
9. To make a determination regarding the child's best interests and advocate for those best interests according to the GAL's understanding of those best interests, regardless of whether the GAL's determination reflects the child's wishes.

A child's interests can be relevant to the GAL's determination of the child's best interests, and the GAL shall weigh the child's wishes according to the child's competence and maturity. Consistent with the law governing attorney-client privilege, the GAL informs the court as to the child's wishes and preference.

The bottom line is what is best for the child and not what one parent or the other may want or think is in the best interests of the child. The GAL, an experienced and trained person, can be very helpful in such high-conflict circumstances.

PARENTING COORDINATOR

A Parenting Coordinator is a trained professional who is appointed by the court for a specified term to help implement parenting time orders and to help resolve disputes that are covered by the order regarding the Parenting Coordinator's appointment. The Parenting Coordinator often faces a very challenging task.

We have had many cases where a Parenting Coordinator was used. Most often, the Parenting Coordinator meets with the parents and with the children, but sometimes the better strategy is for the coordinator to only work with the parents. Every case is different.

In some high-conflict custody cases, the Parenting Coordinator is the one who has to listen to all of the allegations and counter-allegations and sort through them. Recommendations are made and in some situations, the coordinator will be called to testify in court.

Costs can be a factor as well. Again, as with the GAL, the costs of the Parenting Coordinator are the responsibility of the parents. These specially appointed experts can be uniquely helpful.

TAKEAWAYS

Judges, attorneys, and litigants utilize a GAL, a Parenting Coordinator, or both in high-conflict custody and parenting time disputes. Because of the costs involved, they are called in sparingly. However, they are assets that can be utilized in difficult cases. The laws and customs regarding the GAL and Parenting Coordinator will differ from state to state. It is critical that you discuss these issues with your attorney to see if these options are available in your state.

The authors thank family law attorney Delia Miller for her contributions to this chapter.

Notes

CHAPTER 22

RESOLVING YOUR CASE

C

hild custody can be a key part of divorce. It can also be the main issue for married as well as unmarried couples — heterosexual or LGBTQ, or for those who weren't even really a couple because of an extremely brief relationship.

Regardless of circumstances, resolving a case still follows certain patterns. In the nonmarital situation or a post-judgment divorce where custody has become an issue, resolution can be more difficult. The reason is that in a divorce, there can be more moving parts or issues. This results in more of an ability to trade or compromise on some facets in return for attaining one objective or another. With custody and parenting, we cannot forget that the focus is not on what Mom or Dad wants, but what is in the best interests of the child.

SIT DOWN, GET IT DONE

If you can communicate and put whatever brought you to the point of a divorce or a custody battle behind you, the best result is one where the parties can act as two rational adults and sit down to discuss a parenting plan. The key is to focus on what is best for the child or children and not what the parents necessarily want. By focusing on the child's needs and creating a schedule in writing that looks at what makes sense, often a settlement can be achieved.

This would then be written up as an order or agreement that provides the road map for moving forward to the next phase of your lives and that of your children's. Even if you are able to agree on your own, it is critical to at least consult with a family law attorney to make sure that all issues are properly covered. The settlement is then put in writing to become part of a judgment or order of the court. This should be done in accordance with the laws of your state.

TALKING IT OUT

Communication is critical. If the parents and their attorneys can sit down and work out the issues, an agreement can be reached that saves you a lot of money as well as emotional trauma. By focusing on the best interests of your child and creating a plan that makes sense, you will be doing a service for everyone.

The best results of any custody or parenting time dispute are those that are reached without court intervention. Having experienced family law attorneys and psychotherapists to shepherd you through the process and keep you out of court is usually the best result for everyone.

If you are willing to keep an open mind and listen to what the other parent is saying, often a sensible result can be achieved. Keep in mind that with two parents who work, creating a parenting plan around work schedules makes a lot of sense.

We find in our practices that too many people overly focus on the number of overnights that each parent has. In many cases, a 50-50 split from the perspective of one year makes sense. This is where having the advice of an experienced attorney and/or helpful psychologist or other therapist can be especially productive.

MEDIATION

In our state, when a case is not settled, most attorneys and judges will refer a case to a mediator before going to trial. Mediation is an effective process that, in most situations, works. The beauty of it is that you as a parent are directly involved in every step of the process and won't lose control of your life and that of your child or children as you would if you end up in trial.

In many high-conflict cases, we urge everyone to go into early-stage mediation to avert the need to go into litigation. This way, you can get a feeling for the case early on and can intervene where necessary to try to keep it from spinning out of control.

The mediator will establish ground rules for everyone including working on interim parenting time and financial arrangements as the case progresses. The goal is to keep everything moving in a functional manner and to avoid having the litigants participate in many court hearings, which are time-consuming, expensive, stressful, and not necessarily productive.

Typically before a mediation session, each side prepares a mediation summary. Most mediators want a history of the marriage if it is a divorce case. If it is not a divorce, the mediator is wanting to understand the history of the relationship and issues. A good summary should be relevant and brief.

Every mediator has a different style and approach. The mediator will have read the summaries in advance of the mediation session. A mediator should have ideas and suggestions as to what makes sense to help resolve the case, keeping in mind that the focus is to be on the best interests of the child.

Some mediators meet with everyone together in one conference room. Another approach is to have each parent and his or her attorneys in separate conference rooms for a more productive process.

We have found over the years that the mediation summaries often appear farther apart than the parties themselves really are. There is a good reason for this. When you are mediating or going through a mediation session, you never want to have your bottom line out there. If you start with where you want to end up, you will never get what you want. It is critical to always leave some negotiating room. By having everyone separate, getting to the bottom line of what each side really wants and sorting out the issues moves more quickly than if everyone is together.

In many divorce and custody battles, one of the spouses or parents is often in a weaker position. If they are kept in two separate rooms with their attorneys, it helps to level the playing field. It's not unusual for the mediator to spend more time with one side than the other if one parent needs it.

In some cases, a resolution can be achieved in a matter of hours; others may take several sessions as we work on issues. It's not unusual to give homework to the parties in an effort to make sure that the issues being raised can be dealt with productively and rationally. If they cannot be handled at the initial session due to a lack of information, then we will schedule another mediation after the homework has been completed.

We also talk to the attorneys separately and, if asked, will give opinions as to what we think might happen if the case goes through a hearing or trial. The goal is to help everyone focus on what is best for the children and not necessarily what each side wants.

If one side is unsure or is having doubts, sometimes a good solution is to prepare an agreement, and then let both parties have some time to take it home and think about it with his or her attorneys. The danger here is that often there can be buyer's remorse and then the entire settlement can unravel.

It is important for anyone going through a custody or parenting time dispute to look at the big picture, and keep in mind what is in the best interests of the children. By settling in mediation, there is a tremendous savings in attorney fees as well as the emotional cost of actually going to trial.

It is important to remember that there are no winners in a divorce or custody battle. Compromise is always best. A good settlement is one where no one gets everything and neither side is happy — that is the reality of child custody and parenting time issues. You never get to see your child or children all of the time!

WHEN MEDIATION WORKS

Consider this recent complex case in which mediation worked. The father and the mother had been living together and had a little girl who was 1 year old at the time of mediation. When the parties were living together in Michigan, the mother had worked nights and the dad had worked days, which meant he was involved in the daily upbringing of their little girl.

When the case started, the father retained Co-author Henry S. Gornbein a day after the mother had taken the child and moved out of Michigan and relocated to Florida, where she had originally resided and now had obtained employment. The case was properly filed in Michigan and the father's goal was to force the return of the little girl.

Several contentious court hearings and two mediation sessions followed. Between the first and second mediations, the father disclosed that he was exploring the possibility of transferring to Florida and finding work there. He said that he would agree to the move to Florida if he could have his daughter with him 50 percent of the time, with liberal parenting time between Michigan and Florida until the move took place.

At the first mediation session, everyone was in separate rooms. At the beginning of the second session, both parents said that they would like to talk as a group for a while — which they did, but then separated. After several hours, a compromise was reached: once the father moved to Florida, he would have six rather than seven out of 14 overnights during a two-week period, but would also have some additional time during school breaks and vacations.

With compromise, everyone was able to settle and save the acrimony and cost of a trial. The settlement meant they could now put aside their differences, begin to heal, and focus on what was best for raising their daughter. They also agreed to joint legal and physical custody.

The key lesson is that through mediation, the parties were able to control their own destiny and not leave their fates and that of their daughter in the hands of a stranger in a black robe.

COLLABORATIVE LAW

Collaborative law is another option that is growing in popularity. It is used more and more in divorce but can be employed in nonmarital custody disputes as well. Henry S. Gornbein is trained as a collaborative attorney and finds it works well.

The key is that each of the parties hires an attorney who is trained and willing to work in the collaborative process. In some cases, a mediator who is trained collaboratively as well will be involved, along with psychotherapists who are collaboratively trained to work on custody and parenting time issues to help coach the parents through the process with the goal being to work on solutions rather than go to court.

Through a series of meetings with everyone working together, the goal is to fashion a result that makes sense, taking into account the economics of the parties and what is in the best interests of the children.

A key part of collaborative law is that if the process breaks down and a settlement is not reached, the attorneys and other collaboratively trained professionals have to step aside; then if the parties choose to litigate, they have to hire a new team of professionals.

A written collaborative agreement is created at the beginning of the process that spells out the terms of the representation of the parties and sets ground rules from the onset. The result is that there is not only a strong emotional incentive to resolve the case collaboratively, but also an economic one. By having meetings in a controlled collaborative environment with everyone in the same room, a creative solution — too often unlikely to happen in a traditional courtroom setting — can be reached.

Again, the key is keeping control of your lives and those of your children. Every collaborative case Henry has been involved in has been settled without the need for court intervention. The process clearly works.

ARBITRATION

When mediation, negotiation, or a collaborative approach has failed, there is another option: arbitration. This is a legal technique for resolving disputes outside of court in which an arbitrator renders a decision that the parties agree to accept. The arbitrator is normally a lawyer who specializes in family law or a retired judge. The hearings will be in a more formal setting than mediation, with testimony being taken from witnesses and evidence being put on the record as part of the case.

In arbitration, a written agreement is drawn up and signed by the parties and their attorneys. It spells out the terms, duties of the arbitrator, and how formal or informal the process will be. It will list the issues to be arbitrated. For example, if custody is the major issue along with parenting time, this will be listed in the agreement. If child support is an issue, that will be included as well. There will also be a discussion regarding how discovery and evidence will be handled. A court order placing the case into arbitration is also required.

Why go through arbitration and not directly to trial? There are several reasons. Over the years, we have seen cases that should have taken a few hours end up taking several days in court. With arbitration, you set a time and day for the hearing. You then go to the office of the arbitrator and get started. There are no interruptions and you continue for as many hours of a given day as everyone agrees to.

On the other hand, when you go to court, there are always delays. A day in court where you hope to have six or seven hours of trial time actually may turn out to be two or three.

Held a few hours at a time, trials can last for months. I have known judges to start a trial and then after taking some testimony, order the parties back to a mediator.

You can pick your arbitrator, but not your judge. Judges are assigned to your case by a blind draw or similar arrangement from state to state. There are many wonderful judges, but some are not. Take one case where the judge called the attorneys into his chambers before the trial was to start, pulled out a coin and said, "Call it." Others have had biases or preconceived notions that influenced the way they interpreted the facts.

Once you go before a judge, you and the other parent are no longer making the decisions about your lives and those of your children; at that point, a stranger who does not know you and in some cases could not care less about you is deciding about your family and the fate of your children. Is that what you really want?

A trained expert in family law who is arbitrating your case can get to the core issues much faster than many judges can or will. In arbitration, you can set your own rules. You can be as informal or formal as you and your attorneys want. You can set the rules regarding witnesses and the rules of evidence to fit your needs. This is not typical in a formal trial.

While hiring an arbitrator can be costly, the expenses are normally split between the parties. In addition, you can streamline the process through arbitration. A trial that might take a week or more in court can be done in half the time with a skilled arbitrator.

There are some possible disadvantages to arbitration. First, if there is a history of domestic violence in your marriage or relationship, this process may not be right for you. You must be sure that you are fully protected in the event of arbitration if you and/or your children have been victims of domestic violence in your marriage or relationship.

Second, if you are unhappy with the arbitrator's decision, it is much more difficult to appeal an arbitrator's award or ruling than it is to appeal a judge's decision following a hearing or trial.

Before you make a decision on going with arbitration, seek the advice and counsel of your attorney to determine whether arbitration is best for your situation. It is not an easy decision.

GOING TO TRIAL

A very small percentage of the divorces or custody cases we are involved with go to trial. With the filtering process that starts from the informality of a couple sitting down and working out their issues to the opposite extreme of arbitration, very few cases remain to go through an actual trial.

Sometimes a trial is started and then after a few hours or a day in court, the judge has the parties sit in a jury room and pressures everyone to settle. That can work.

Sometimes having a moment in court to get issues off of your chest will work wonders and then a case that previously could not be settled will be resolved.

When a divorce or custody case goes to trial, though, it is because some attorneys refuse to look at solutions or are unable to properly advise their clients. Also, in some situations — especially those with complicated custody or change of domicile issues where no matter what is tried, a settlement cannot be reached — a trial becomes the last and only resort. And it may become the only option in situations when there are emotional or mental problems on the part of one or both parents. When anger and bitterness are so out of control that you and your spouse or partner cannot let go and move on, refusing all other solutions and attempts at an agreement along the way, then a trial may be inevitable.

That is unfortunate. Trials are emotionally draining for everyone involved — for the attorneys, for you and the other parent or spouse, for your children to the extent that they are thrown into the morass, and for any psychologists or other experts who testify.

We strongly believe that children should never appear in court. They should never be required to testify in a trial or hearing, period. In Michigan, judges considering custody issues talk to children privately in their chambers. They keep such discussions confidential to protect the children. In another chapter, we share a peek behind the scenes of what goes on when a judge talks to the children in a custody or parenting time dispute.

We have talked to many judges over the years, and they all agree that they would rather have the parties make their own decisions than for the judge to be put in the position of having to rule. It is hard to be a Solomon! Judges do not know you, and after they hear what you have to say in open court, they might not like you. You will most likely be unhappy with the results.

Once you testify about everything that is wrong with your spouse or the other parent — once you tell the court and the world, so to speak, what a horrible parent he or she is, you can never take these words back. No matter what the result is, you will have to parent your children and raise them together in some fashion. Having a public record of what is being said makes it that much harder to heal and move forward.

If you go to trial, be prepared. Make sure that every issue is covered in advance. If you do end up testifying in court, be brief and to the point. Do not ramble. By all means, never lie in court. Fibbing on even a minor issue will destroy your credibility before the judge on anything else.

ABOUT ATTORNEYS

We have already mentioned the importance of being represented by the right attorney — that there are attorneys who are problem-solvers and others who create problems. You do not want the latter.

Some attorneys are always in trial. There are several reasons for this. One is that they will churn a file to create huge and often unnecessary costs and fees. Clients are encouraged to be more emotional and fight over every issue — a scorched-earth tactic that hurts everyone. It sure won't help your children!

A good lawyer will give advice and help you evaluate all of your options as you go through the legal process. This is critical. You want your attorney to also step back and look at the big picture. You do not want to be represented by someone who just sees everything your way and helps lead you down the path to disaster. You want — and are paying for — sound legal advice. You need an advocate, but don't want a lawyer who just follows you without offering opinions and advice based on his or her experience and knowledge of the legal process.

A good attorney will try to take control of a case as early as possible. Discuss and raise the issues so that you can start looking for solutions. Your attorney should contact the other counsel to discuss ways to proceed without just rushing off to the courthouse. Too many attorneys will file motions and go to court rather than meeting first to see if issues can be resolved or at least narrowed — this is so important no matter how little or much money you have and what issues there may be regarding your children.

Talk first and go to court as a last resort. Never lose sight that the key is what is in the best interests of your children. We cannot emphasize that too strongly!

THE LAST WORD

We have been involved in many custody trials. We have had clients who would not listen to our advice or compromise. We have seen these same clients devastated after a judge took away or greatly limited the time that they could spend with their children. We have seen people get the worst possible result because they refused to listen to our advice.

Having your day in court should be a last resort — when all else fails. A divorce trial is too often a sign of failure — by you and by your attorneys. Wouldn't you rather compromise and be able to put the money that you would be spending on attorney fees toward your children's college education?

TAKEAWAYS

It is important that you understand all of your options as you navigate the legal system regarding any child-related issues that you might have. These steps include direct negotiations, mediation, collaborative law, arbitration, and last — going to trial.

Notes

Notes

CHAPTER 23

THE JUDICIAL INTERVIEW: REASONABLE PREFERENCE OF THE CHILD

In child custody cases, one of the important issues that must be considered by a judge is the reasonable preference of the child. Most children don't want to choose. They just want their parents to stop fighting.

The law of many states requires that a judge talk to the child or children during a child custody dispute to help make a determination consistent with their best interests. Children are typically interviewed after all of the other data has been reviewed. We are often asked at what age a child can decide with which parent the child wants to live.

There are no easy answers to that question. Results will vary from state to state — even from judge to judge. There usually is no specific age; everything is decided on the facts and issues that are relevant in each case.

We once surveyed the judges in the three most populous counties in Michigan regarding issues of the judicial interview of children in custody matters. Of the 23 judges who were surveyed, 14 provided extensive written responses. The questions and their responses follow.

1. What is the youngest age that you will talk to a child?

Ages widely ranged from 4 to 10 or 11, with the majority saying 5 or 6. Many judges perceived that the verbal skills of most 5- or 6-year-olds represent the minimum age for obtaining reliable information. This also is consistent with some research.

2. Do you have any other person present when you interview a child?

Most judges reported that they always have someone present when they interview a child. Few video record.

3. If so, who is present with you?

The answers ranged widely, including the court reporter, other staff, the case GAL (Guardian Ad Litem), research attorney, or a family counselor. In some cases, a secretary took notes for the confidential court file.

4. Are there any specific questions that you ask a child? If so, what are they?

This elicited a wide variety of responses. Often questions were asked about the child's interests to help break the ice and make the child comfortable, as well as general life questions. Some judges explain that it is the judge's job to help their parents when the parents don't agree.

Some judges find it is important to find out about pets, living arrangements, school, friends, siblings, music, sports, arts, video games, and also in general how the child feels their life is going.

Sometimes children are asked if they know the difference between telling the truth and a lie.

Some judges explore the issue of whether or not a child has been coached.

Most children and almost all teenagers want the judicial interview over quickly. Children often are asked what they do at each parent's home. Who do they go to with their problems and successes? Who picks them up from school when they are sick?

Children are often asked to tell the judge one thing they like about each parent. **Other questions that judges ask children in their private offices may include:**

Where do you go to school?

How are your grades?

Do you play sports?

Are you in clubs/activities?

Tell me some good things about each of your parents — is there anything you want to tell me, and is there anything I can help you with?

Who lives at Mom/Dad's house? How do you get along with everyone there? What do you do for fun there? Do you have your own bedroom?

What about discipline? Schoolwork?

What activities do you like to do? Who does them with you? Is there anything else you "are supposed" to tell me?

Who gets you up in the morning; prepares breakfast; gets you to school; gets you home; helps with homework; goes to soccer/baseball?

What are your chores; nighttime routine; bedtime; weekends?

5. Do you ever ask children to state their preference for which parent with whom they would like to live?

Most judges ask open-ended questions in this regard. Some judges put it this way: "If you could live anywhere you want, or have any schedule with your parents, what would it be?"

Judges typically reassure children that their responses are confidential and won't be disclosed.

Judges make clear that the judge is responsible for the decision, not the child: "I let them know I'm helping Mom and Dad decide how much time at each home."

6. At what age does a child's preference carry significant weight in your decision-making process?

The responses of the judges varied widely, though many indicated the minimum age should be based on the particular child's maturity and personal characteristics. The minimum end for some judges was ages 9-12 and the minimum age for other judges was ages 15-17.

7. How important is the preference of a teenager?

Every family presents a unique set of circumstances. The older the child, the better the child's ability to express a preference.

Many judges feel teenagers' wishes are significant, especially if they are able to articulate solid reasons for their preference. Some judges want to understand the incentives at the different homes that may be influencing those preferences

— i.e., girlfriend/boyfriend, staying out late, driving, cell phone, freedom, one parent more lenient, etc.

As for other issues, judges recommend that children not be coached, since that is not honest and puts pressure on the child. Children rarely say what their parents think they will — they are usually very direct.

The judge can usually detect when a child has been coached — a major negative for the coaching parent: "Once I asked a child if there was anything else he was 'supposed' to tell me. He ticked off all his points on his fingers to make sure he covered them all!"

Judges also stated that they do not care how old a child is — they are not going to allow a teenager to tell them how to run their courtrooms. The purpose of the judicial interview is to get to know the child, glean needed information, and help the parties settle the case.

TAKEAWAYS

Sometimes judges interview children about their lives and preferences. The expressed preference of your child can be an important issue in your custody case — just how important depends on their age and the facts of the case. Remember that your child's preference may not be what you think it is. It is important not to coach your child before speaking to a judge or an evaluator. Each situation is different.

Notes

_____

_____

_____

_____

_____

_____

_____

_____

_____

_____

_____

_____

_____

_____

_____

_____

_____

_____

_____

_____

_____

_____

_____

_____

_____

_____

CHAPTER 24

PERSPECTIVES FROM THE BENCH

T he authors had the honor and pleasure of interviewing the Honorable Kathleen M. McCarthy, Presiding Judge for the Wayne Circuit Court-Family Division, for this chapter.

The jurisdiction of Wayne County includes the City of Detroit in addition to 41 other cities. Wayne County is a large metropolitan court — in fact, it is the eighth largest in the country. Each judge has approximately 1,000 active cases and is responsible for approximately 25,000 post-judgment cases. This chapter is excerpted from that interview, which focuses on the role of the judge in custody and parenting time matters.

The goal of court proceedings regarding custody and parenting time is to encourage parents to work together to resolve childrearing disputes. The process varies in different legal jurisdictions. Often, mediation is tried first. If this is not successful, a settlement conference with the judge is tried. If that is unsuccessful, then a court trial may be necessary. The court is ready, willing, and able to do this. However, everyone involved with the legal process knows a trial is not the best way to resolve family conflicts, particularly custody and parenting time disputes. The trial can entrench parties to their positions, air a family's dirty laundry, and requires the children to be involved in the court process. Trials are to be avoided, if possible.

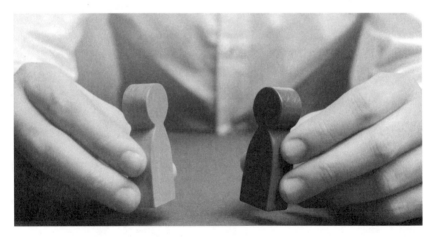

There are multiple problems with a family court trial, which is costly to the parties in many ways. First, there are the financial expenses: preparation, depositions, discovery, mediation, and the trial itself can result in exorbitant legal fees. Second, trial and trial preparation are time-intensive and very stressful on all involved.

Trials themselves can last anywhere from hours to many days. They also do not bring out the best characteristics in the participants, often focusing on each party's worst qualities.

Most problematic, such trials disrupt, complicate, intensify, and typically worsen already strained parental relationships, since battles over custody and parenting time by that point are emotionally intense and adversarial. People often have a hard time healing after a custody trial.

More important, children do not benefit from their parents being involved in what often are bitter, adversarial legal proceedings. They are put in the middle. Nobody wins.

A high percentage of couples in custody conflicts, particularly in Wayne County, are never-married parties who typically have not developed the depth of trust that many married couples had at one point. In some cases, never-married couples with custody and parenting time difficulties may not even know the other parent very well. This makes resolving parenting time and custody cases even more difficult. *(Please see Chapter 12 on never-married parents.)*

SELF-REPRESENTATION

In recent years, there has been a significant increase in the number of parents representing themselves in the court process and trial proceedings instead of hiring an attorney. People representing themselves do not typically have the tools that attorneys possess. This includes knowing and understanding the legal process, filing pleadings in conformance with rules and statutes, and entering orders that comply with those court rules and statutes.

More importantly, an attorney provides an unbiased review of the law as applied to the facts of a party's case. An unrepresented parent must prepare a factual and legal summary of the case (brief), bring relevant documents, provide relevant facts, and correctly refer to applicable law. If witnesses are presented, they need to be relevant and prepared to address specific issues involved at trial. Parents need to come to court organized, ready to reconcile their facts with the law.

Lawyers act as a buffer between the parties. They are educated in the law and know proper procedures and court rules. They understand how to appropriately apply the facts of a case to the law, and how to present facts to the court. Attorneys are routinely better organized and prepared.

Attorneys have an understanding of the legal process and can stipulate to reports or records helpful to decide relevant issues, often shortening trial time. The court is neutral, it is not a fact finder, but rather deals with the facts that are presented. Obtaining an attorney greatly helps litigants move through the court processes and get matters resolved quicker.

KNOW THE RULES

In addition to knowing and understanding the facts and the law, litigants need to know that there are rules in every courthouse. Both oral and physical presentation give the jurist an impression as to a party's behavior as well as conduct inside and outside of the courtroom.

That means presenting yourself in court properly attired — in business-casual clothing such as dress pants and tops, or suits, normal-length skirts and dresses. Do not wear jeans, a tee-shirt, or a baseball cap.

Proper decorum in the courtroom in oral presentation is also an important show of respect to the jurist and legal process. Participants are expected to be appropriate, courteous, and polite, including waiting their turn to talk. Demonstrating respect and conducting one's self with dignity is important if litigants want the judge to take them seriously and give their arguments thoughtful consideration.

Truthfulness is also vitally important. Participants are sworn to tell the truth. Sometimes character witnesses can be helpful. Such witnesses may provide information as a result of having spent time with the parent or with the parent and the child. But if the court determines that a parent or witness is untruthful, it is less likely to rule in their favor.

Successful cases must be built on credibility. Jurists are real people with real lives, so truth and directness are critical. If you are not truthful inside a courtroom, your credibility — and, probably, your case — will be damaged.

ALL ABOUT THE CHILDREN

Whether parents are represented by an attorney or themselves, the focus in any hearing is the same, by law: the best interests of the children.

Courts follow laws referred to as statutes having to do with child custody and parenting time and so must consider 12 factors in making their determination.*

One factor mandates examination of the home, school, and community record of the child. This often gives important information to the jurist regarding the investment each parent has made in parenting. It demonstrates the stability or instability of a parent or an environment, and how well children are navigating their own lives within that environment.

Judges consider how well the family is functioning. Examples: How does the parent-child relationship work? Are health issues looked after? Who goes to the doctor with a child? Are immunizations up-to-date? How is the child's hygiene maintained? Are healthy meals served? Is schoolwork done? Who attends parent-teacher conferences? Are there bedtimes? How much time does each parent spend with the child, and what is the content of that contact? Does each parent know the friends of the child? Are there limits on television and video games? Is the child shielded from anger issues and violence? Is there drug or alcohol use or abuse by either parent? If so, is the child shielded from such abuse — and from any chaos or parental discord within the family?

Often a court will seek information from traditional sources, or technology may provide some answers. Police reports, report cards, school attendance records, and medical records are examples of the former. Of the latter, text messages, Facebook posts, and phone records are among the sources commonly examined. Facebook and social media can also give the court glimpses into the personal lives of the parents outside of court, including who their friends are, how they dress, and how they behave in real life. They can even provide insight into whether or not a parent drinks excessively, smokes, or takes drugs.

In most cases that head to trial, judges interview the children in custody and parenting time disputes. In some states, such an interview is mandatory. Generally the clarity and credibility of what most children say increases at about age 7. In that interview, a judge often explores what a typical day is like for the child and who that child seems better bonded with. Jurists also look for signs that a child has been coached by one parent or the other. Needless to say, seasoned judges can reliably perceive if coaching has taken place and do not look favorably on the coaching parent.

As for the assistance of professionals, a judge can direct that an attorney (Guardian Ad Litem) be appointed to represent the interests of a child during a divorce or post-divorce issue. This can help keep the focus on the best interests of the child rather than on parental wrangling. A judge can also appoint a parenting coordinator (mental health professional or attorney) to work with the parents on resolving parental disputes. The goal of the court typically includes trying to help the parties learn how to get along better regarding the child.

Courts sometimes appoint psychologists to interview and psychologically test parents and children (different interviews and different testing with children). This includes reviewing collateral information and in-home and in-office observations. *(Please see Chapter 25 on psychological assessment in custody matters.)*

Courts can be particularly concerned for the welfare of children not only if there has been criminal behavior by a parent such as domestic violence, but also if there have been substance abuse issues going on in the home. The latter often reflects an orientation by the parent or parents to avoid and escape life challenges — and of course, raising children can be challenging, and substance abuse occurring in the home can place kids in danger.

Another challenge for courts regarding decisions involving custody and parenting time often relates to allegations of parental alienation. *(Please see Chapter 11 on parental alienation.)* Parental alienation is a complex and multidimensional dynamic that develops between a parent and child within the context of custody disputes. Sometimes alienating behavior can be intentional;

sometimes it is a product of poor parent-child relationships. The main goal of the court is to protect children, and this can be a difficult issue for the jurist to sort out and understand.

In some cases, allegations that a parent is alienating a child from the other parent are actually based on absenteeism or lack of caring behavior by the reportedly alienated parent. However, some allegations are rooted more in the spousal relationship itself and unresolved fears that a parent harbors toward the other parent, either realistically or not, and have nothing really to do with the child-parent relationship.

In addition, parental alienation can also involve directed efforts to distort the parent-child relationship and diminish trust so that even positive efforts on the part of the parent are viewed with skepticism, if not disdain.

SUBJECT TO CHANGE

A court must also make decisions regarding changes in parenting time as children grow older or if a parent's circumstances change, such as whether or not a mom or dad should be able to move away with a child due to job relocations or remarriages. When it comes to a move, the court must take into account the nature of the relationship between the child and the parent who is not moving, the age of the child, the proposed distance between homes, any patterns of abuse or neglect, and any monetary or other basis of the request to move the child away.

In cases involving changes in parenting time, other conditions need to be assessed, such as a child's ability to participate in sporting events and potential access to friends or extended family if the child is close to them.

One of the newer areas of law involving families and custody cases is the emerging law on same-sex marriages, custody rights, and redefining who and what a parent is. The rights of the LGBTQ community are being redefined regarding custody and parenting time in most jurisdictions.

TAKEAWAYS

Many of the issues considered by and decided on by family courts are complex. They involve a multitude of variables including the credibility of the parties. The court must always focus on the best interests of the children while considering the rights and responsibilities of their parents. Clearly, parties working together, putting aside their needs, and presenting agreed-upon resolutions is always in a child's best interests and the most positive resolution a family court can make. However, when that is not possible, the court must review the evidence and documentation before it, apply the law to the facts of the case, and make the best decision they can. As many more litigants are choosing to represent themselves, the best decisions can be compromised due to a lack of evidence or facts being properly presented to the jurist. Further, as many more litigants are having children outside of a marital structure and live lives very separate and apart from the other parent, custody and parenting time decisions will remain a difficult issue before the trial courts.

(Please see Chapter 22 for more on parenting time.)

*Michigan Child Custody statute MCL.700.22(a)

Notes

Notes

CHAPTER

THE PSYCHOLOGICAL EVALUATION

Most courts decide child custody and parenting time disputes using the standard of "best interests of the child." The meaning of this concept is described in the wording of the law in each state. Judgments about the different parts of the law (often called a statute, since it is part of a larger law) are typically determined by a decision of the court that can be made by the judge or a referee, who possesses most of the powers of — and is appointed by — the judge.

Most often custody decisions are made during discussions between spouses or later communications between the representing attorneys. But when spouses or attorneys representing the parties do not agree, the matter may be referred for psychological evaluation. Psychological evaluations are performed by psychologists who are trained and experienced, and who by licensing law are able to do psychological testing.

In a child custody evaluation, typically the judge or referee appoints the psychologist to assist. The evaluating psychologist follows the same legal "best interests" standards as the judge in making his or her findings. Sometimes courts want just a summary description from the psychologist based on the information in that case. Most often, the court is looking for recommendations about actions to take regarding custody and parenting time.

Often a state's "best interests" statute calls for evaluation of the emotional attachment of the child to each parent, the history of involvement of each parent with the child, the mental and physical health of each parent, possible domestic violence, and the wishes of the child (depending on the child's age) regarding custody. Sometimes there are additional facets to be considered. One of the benefits of evaluation is that most often, the attorneys can much more effectively work with the parties and resolve the matter without a trial.

Typically the court will order a child custody evaluation if the parties cannot agree or if there are apparently controversial or troublesome aspects to the functioning of one or both parents, including but not limited to: substance abuse, mental health issues, violence or other instabilities, irregularities, or unpredictable behaviors by one or both parents.

Psychological evaluations are involved in perhaps 10 percent or fewer of divorces involving children. However, if a custody evaluation is called for, it becomes very, very important.

PSYCHOTHERAPIST VS. EVALUATOR

The court will typically order the evaluation, indicating who is to be evaluated and for what purpose and specifying what it needs from the evaluation. An evaluator should have no prior involvement with the parties in the role of psychotherapist or as a consultant to either party. Evaluators should not have dual or multiple roles. In fact, they should have no role conflict at all, since a psychotherapist is an advocate for the person in psychotherapy, and an evaluator is an impartial investigator and reporter — not an advocate or intervenor.

For example, psychotherapists may feel they know the child, parent, or family and what is best. But a psychotherapist does not have the sort of impartial information nor the comprehensive objective information that an evaluator collects, so it is actually unethical for the psychotherapist to offer a custody recommendation.

An evaluation must be done with objectivity. During the evaluation process, the evaluator does not offer suggestions or direction. It is an evaluator's responsibility to provide a safe and neutral environment for the parties to express themselves openly and freely.

WHAT IS CONFIDENTIALITY?

The work done by the evaluating psychologist is confidential. Confidentiality is the basis of the work of psychologists, whether doing evaluations or psychotherapy. Confidentiality is somewhat similar to privacy, a right alluded to in the Fourth Amendment of the Constitution. The right of privacy allows or entitles each person to make decisions about sharing his or her private thoughts, feelings, or information in many circumstances.

Confidentiality is a professional standard of conduct with an ethical and a legal basis. It requires a practitioner (here a psychologist, a mental health practitioner) to not divulge information obtained. There are exceptions, such as when there is potential for harm.

In a court-ordered psychological evaluation, the psychologist will have the parent sign a release of information for him/herself and for any children in legal custody. The release waives confidentiality and allows the psychologist to inform whomever the parent designates to receive the results of the evaluation.

Usually permission is requested by the psychologist for the parent to allow transmission of confidential information to the court, to the two attorneys, and to the lawyer the court has appointed to represent the child(ren), if applicable. The process is usually called "release of confidentiality." Such permission may not be required if the court has formally ordered evaluation.

The structural advantage of a psychological evaluation includes focused work by a trained professional who can impartially gather information and apply it to the context that is useful to the judge or referee. In a sense, the psychologist is an advocate for the child. Unlike a psychotherapist, the role of custody evaluator is impartial, focused solely on assisting the court.

Typically there is a written report of the evaluation. In some cases, if there is a trial, the psychologist may testify about those findings.

LEGAL PRIVILEGE

A related concept is "privilege," which deals with protection under the law that is granted to some relationships. Privilege involves a person not being forced to divulge information in legal proceedings. The client "holds" the privilege and can "waive" it if he or she chooses, as in relationships of trust such as doctor-patient or lawyer-client.

Sometimes the structure of a court-ordered evaluation provides for that privilege to be waived for the purpose of the court hearing, and usually the privilege is waived so information can be released to the court and two attorneys. The release may be stated in the court order, and it would be stated in the document of release of confidentiality to be signed by each parent. The characteristics of each custody case may impose limits or rules on privilege — every case can be different. Parents who hold legal custody of their children hold the privilege on their behalf.

States often place limits on professional confidentiality, such as when there are threats to the safety of a client or someone else or in situations of suspected child or elder abuse. Mental health professionals may be mandated to report suspected abuse in some situations. If discovered during an evaluation, the safety of the child supersedes the process of the evaluation and the evaluator is obligated to report.

Typically, psychological evaluations gather information of different types and apply it to the components of the child custody statute for that state or jurisdiction.

WHAT TO EXPECT

Psychological evaluation is challenging, and it can be especially complex in custody evaluation situations. Individuals in the process of contested divorce are under stress. The evaluator should try to discern and distinguish between divorce-induced stress, with its likely adversarial aspects, and the stable, longer-term characteristics of the individual.

To start, the evaluator may spend at least 30 minutes carefully explaining the purpose and components of the evaluation. It is important that the purpose and scope are understood by the parent. This establishes an orientation of cooperation with the evaluator and clarifies expectations for the parent. Parents know what to expect for themselves and for their children and that there is a definite time commitment, especially for the parents.

The psychological tests are generally described, and parents learn that their children will be taking very different tests. The experience of their children can be addressed at that time. Initially, a signed permission to release information form is obtained.

Parents often are instructed to tell the child or children to be evaluated that the psychologist knows Mom and Dad and is trying to see how things are going, for the purpose of helping them get along better. The child needs to be comfortable, or become comfortable, with the psychologist. The parent can tailor the description of what will go on with the psychologist based on the age of the child. It is important that a parent not "prep" a child for an evaluation. Children should be directed only to be honest and express what they think and feel to the examiner. They can be told that they probably will like talking.

Sometimes children are resistant before they come to the first appointment. Younger children are more interested in the description than teens, for example, many of whom can be blasé or bothered by the imposition on their time. It is important for the parent to facilitate a positive relationship between the psychologist and the child.

Most children respond well to a trained professional who is friendly, relaxed, and unhurried with them. They visibly relax after a few minutes, once their apprehensions have been allayed. They appear to perceive the environment to be responsive and supportive — not as "putting them in the middle," as their parents may have done. The focus of most of the interview is on the child and his/her experiences, reactions, and hopes.

In our experience, negative reactions by children have been extremely rare and are seen mostly in teenagers not wanting to be bothered in any way regarding the problems of their parents. In fact, many younger children ask if they can return at the end of the last evaluation appointment.

WHY SO MANY SOURCES?

A child custody psychological evaluation needs to collect multiple sources of information. Multiple sources can increase reliability. For that reason, the information can involve interview, observation, collateral such as contact with other professionals, and psychological testing.

This can be broad and take the form of the evaluator reviewing court orders, school records, medical records, inpatient psychiatric or substance abuse treatment, outpatient psychotherapy or substance abuse treatment, police or probation officer information, child protective agency information, or other materials.

Psychotherapist phone interviews may take place. The evaluator may interview all individuals besides the parent and children who live in either residence. New spouse or cohabitating partner information can be important. Sometimes grandparents are interviewed. Permission to ask for information from other professional sources is requested in writing from each parent.

One value of collateral information and contacts besides providing a context is that it can confirm or contradict statements provided by the contesting parties.

INTERVIEW TOPICS

Part of a psychological evaluation involves several hours of individual interviews of each parent. Interviews with the child (or children) also take place.

Typically the parents are conjointly interviewed with a focus on childrearing — not on the marriage and its problems and shortcomings. Questions asked of adults are sometimes difficult because of the experiences during the course of the divorce.

That is not the case with children. Their interviews are age appropriate and specifically tailored to make them comfortable and to encourage open disclosure. Such interviews should be conducted by mental health professionals trained in and skilled at working with children. Most often, preschool-age children are not interviewed. The results of the interviews are stated in the report.

In addition, one or more observation appointments usually take place with each parent separately and the children. Typically one appointment takes place in the examiner's office and some evaluators do additional assessment in the parental residence, whether the parents cohabit or not. If there is involvement with Child Protective Services because of allegations against one of the parents, there must be clear agreement with the appropriate parties that observation is wise. Also, careful judgment must be used in situations in which a parent has not seen a child for months or years. Again, these results are stated in the report.

ABOUT PSYCHOLOGICAL TESTING

A psychological test is a sampling of behavior and personality — a snapshot in time of the functioning of a person. Designed to be objective and assess standardized samples of behavior, such tests are selected to give an independent representation of typical feelings and behaviors.

In custody evaluations, psychological tests need to demonstrate scientifically that they measure what they say they measure — that they are valid. They also need to demonstrate that they produce consistent or accurate results — that they are reliable.

Tests should also be based on norms, i.e., scores produced should be comparable to scores of others who have taken the test, so the meaningfulness of the individual's score can be examined relative to the scores others have produced. The tests used in custody evaluations have been given to thousands of people, including during the process of being constructed.

There are two main aspects of the evaluation. One is to assess each individual. Another evaluates relationships — between the adults, between the children (and any stepchildren), and between parent(s) and children.

There are all sorts of psychological tests, but in custody evaluations, personality is usually a major focus. Tests are selected in terms not only of an evaluation regarding custody, but can be tailored to examine specific other issues such as substance abuse or domestic violence. Although some tests exploring psychopathology are typically administered, the focus is on parenting.

Adults are primarily evaluated for personality functioning. Children are evaluated for their personality functioning and also regarding intellectual and academic functioning, in part to explore the effects of the divorce on those aspects of their functioning. Personality can be described in many ways, including as a description of the individual characteristics of a person and how those characteristics combine to produce behavior that is observable and measurable.

Assessment of a child occurs in the context of seeing how they are psychologically developing. Children of different ages are at different stages of development.

With children, intellectual functioning often is assessed by an individual test of intelligence. One value in assessing intelligence is to examine if the stress of divorce is also affecting the child's cognitive functioning. Academic achievement should be assessed for the same reason. The child's academic and behavioral records should also be evaluated.

There are neither right nor wrong responses to personality tests or measures. Personality measures attempt to describe the most important parts of personality functioning. Objective tests call for a structured response, true-false, or multiple choice — more typically used with adults. Many objective measures are inappropriate for use with children because of the required reading level. Responses are samples. Scores fall along dimensions.

The cumulative scores of individuals to the test produce scores on certain dimensions of personality, whether pathological dimensions such as anxiety or depression or otherwise in other dimensions of more day-to-day functioning, like openness to experience or conscientiousness. An individual's scores are compared to norms.

Projective tests are more indirect methods and deal with more open-ended responses, often responses to ambiguous stimuli. Responses are more correlates of feelings, attitudes, motives, conflicts, and dynamics. Projective test results are based on understanding ways the individual constructs reality, which is viewed as a measure of their psychological functioning. The responses typically are coded for scoring patterns that may be compared to norms that are of a different kind than with objective tests. There may be more inference and interpretation with projective measures than with objective test results, where the skill is more in the integration of different sorts of data.

Questionnaires are sometimes used regarding the life history of each parent. They are more commonly used regarding parenting behaviors or problematic behaviors displayed by children. Some measures are given to parents as well as to teachers regarding a child's behavior.

THE RESULTS

Most people want to look good on psychological testing in custody cases. They feel that "looking good" will help achieve their desired custody outcome.

Most psychological tests have validity scales that measure the extent to which an individual may be distorting responses or reflecting a response set or test attitude. Many of these validity scales also identify random or careless responding patterns.

A common tendency is for a person being evaluated to present themselves in a defensive, overly guarded fashion. When they are overly cautious about revealing themselves, this is at cross purposes from what the test is designed to do: give full and accurate information to the psychologist.

Another tendency is for an individual to present him/herself in an unrealistically favorable light, minimizing common human frailties. A small amount of this may be anticipated in custody cases because each person wants a positive outcome. However, most tests can measure the extent to which a person is likely doing this. If people do this with a heavy hand — and they may not clearly realize the extent to which they are doing it — they are at risk of invalidating the results. Besides being unhelpful and contrary to the spirit of producing good information, it could end up being a negative for their case.

The most constructive approach while taking psychological tests is to trust in the process. Try to answer each question candidly, in accordance with actual thoughts, feelings, and behavior — not with what one might think would be desirable or expected or might look positive or anything else. To a psychologist, candid responses usually are persuasive responses.

In addition to the results of the tests themselves, psychological testing can be used to generate hypotheses regarding collateral information such as reports of professionals and others that are viewed using psychological test results.

The results of the psychological testing are stated in the report. Sometimes scores are also presented, but the focus is on reporting personality characteristics, patterns, and trends. The report may discuss the implication of those findings to the custody dispute at hand, and also could shed light on specific allegations that have been made.

Skill and experience are important in interpreting and using psychological test results. The context also is important. Special circumstances such as mental illness, domestic violence, substance abuse, or specific marital or parent-child communication challenges and problems may call for additional tests on occasion.

The report typically is sent to the court and often to the attorneys. If people represent themselves in the court process, then often the psychologist sends copies of the report to the judge to decide upon the distribution. Evaluations are not intended for the participants.

TAKEAWAYS

Judges give the parties the opportunity to settle without trial by ordering child custody evaluations. It is an opportunity that is best embraced by the parties with a straightforward and candid attitude during evaluation and a positive, settlement-oriented approach to the process afterward. Settlement, if possible, is in the best interests of the children, and psychological evaluations can be helpful.

Most often, the result of the evaluation and report is that the attorneys can much more effectively work with the parties and resolve the matter without a trial. We very highly doubt that anyone familiar with child custody trials would disagree that trials are expensive and stressful. Most importantly, they are disruptive to future relationships between the parties. When custody trials are over, they are not really over since the intensity, animosity, frustrations, and related negative feelings dissipate very slowly, if they do at all.

Notes

Notes

CHAPTER **26**

CHILD CUSTODY & SUPPORT

Whether children are the result of marriage or if the parents never married, child support is an issue that must be resolved as part of the settlement of a custody-related case.

Once custody has been determined, including the number of overnights that the child or children will spend with each parent, a formula specific to your state will be applied to determine the amount of child support to be paid or received.

The formula includes both parents' incomes from all sources including wages, money that is income but goes into your IRA or 401(k) investment accounts, income from disability insurance, unemployment compensation, and Social Security.

The formula will look at the income from each parent as well as the number of children and the number of overnights that the children spend with each parent. Child support is not doubled for each of your children, but is generally based on a type of sliding scale formula. The child support formulas also include medical insurance and uninsured medical expenses for your children.

These formulas are easily accessible online in every state. You can obtain this information yourself or through a local attorney.

The easiest cases for determining the amount and setting child support are where both parents earn a paycheck from a company where all of their income is reported. The most difficult would be when one parent is self-employed or works in a business where a lot of the income is not being reported. These are the cases that give attorneys and the courts nightmares.

In some circumstances, a lifestyle analysis is employed to determine child support. Here, having a knowledgeable attorney can be critical. We have seen cases where a $300,000 house was purchased in cash, but the tax returns only showed an annual income of $50,000. Often, accountants are brought in when the income stream is hidden and complicated.

Payment of child support is normally done through the court system, typically through state-ordered funds or the arm of the court that deals with divorce involving minor children.

Once child support is determined, it is normally reviewed every three years. At any time, either party can request a modification based on changes in circumstances that can include the loss of a job, a reduction in earnings, or a tremendous increase in income.

FACTORS IN SUPPORT

The more overnights each parent has, the less child support will be paid. To some extent, there is a balancing act between income and overnights.

If each parent has a comparable amount of income and share custody equally, there will be little or no child support. This is based on the rationale that each parent is supporting the children when they are with that parent.

On the other hand, if the parent who does not have a lot of overnights with the children has a much greater income than the parent who has the children most of the time, child support will be much greater.

When our client is the father and the major wage earner who also wants as many overnights as possible with the children, we suggest this trade-off: In exchange for more time with the children, he is willing to forgo a substantial reduction in child support so that the economics, at least to some degree, can be kept out of the equation.

Every situation is different, but as parents, you should avoid using child support as an economic weapon in your divorce or custody case. Sadly, we have seen and been involved in many cases where people are fighting about the number of overnights and seeking more time solely because it means paying less child support. The reality is that it is costly to raise a child and unless you are in a very high-income situation, the expenses are much greater than the amount of child support paid.

Over the years, some clients have asked if they can require their soon-to-be ex-spouse to document where the money for child support is going. The answer is no. In the first place, it is impossible to determine where all of the money for support is going and in the second place, no court will allow such micromanagement.

Think of what child support is intended to cover: food, clothing, a portion of the mortgage payment or rent, part of the utilities, part of the costs of a car along with gas, maintenance, and insurance, as well as entertainment and all of the endless incidentals that go hand in hand with raising kids.

Too many people will not let go and move on, and child support can become a prime example of that. Do not try to micromanage your former spouse to try to determine where your child support is going. It will do you no good.

The tragedy of most divorces is that when there is a split, too often there is not enough money to go around. But as we often remind clients, support is for your children. Before you become entrenched in a battle over support, remember that you want your child or children to be supported. Your children are caught in the middle of your divorce to begin with — you do not want them to go without the basic necessities.

In most states, child support usually ends when children reach the age of majority — 18 — or finish high school, whichever is later. It is important to talk to your attorney or check the laws in your state for more specific information.

BEYOND SUPPORT

After the necessities, there are other expenses associated with raising children that will need to be addressed. When you are contemplating or going through a divorce or custody dispute, it is important to sit down with your spouse or significant other and discuss how these items will be handled going forward. If not, be sure to raise them with your attorney so that they will be part of the negotiations and ultimate settlement. In some states, courts will not order payment for extracurricular activities; in others, they may.

In many cases, we may negotiate a separate paragraph to address sharing of costs for extracurricular activities over and above child support. These can include expenses for pursuits like dance, music lessons, and sports. Some activities are inexpensive, but when you get into situations such as hockey, dance, or figure skating, the costs can become tremendous. Boy Scouts, Girl Scouts, religious classes, and ceremonies can be counted in those extracurricular expenses. The list can be endless and these are just a few of the many possibilities.

Other child-related expenses that should be discussed include school if there is parochial or private schooling involved. Summer camps are often discussed and can be included as part of an overall financial settlement. Day care is another component. These are normally addressed as part of the child support formula.

As for college expenses, they can be part of the divorce settlement in some states and can even be ordered by the trial judge. In Michigan, they cannot be ordered by the court.

We have negotiated many cases over the years where there is an agreement reached for either a sharing of college-related expenses or for one parent to pay part or all of the college costs. As long as they are part of the final negotiated settlement and divorce or custody decree, they are fully enforceable by the court and typically consist of tuition, room, board, and books.

In one case, college expenses were covered, but the college was not specified. That turned out to be a huge surprise for the husband, who had agreed to pay them. The child was accepted at an extremely expensive Ivy League university and the father had to pay the tab.

To avoid this type of problem, it is wise to include language that the costs of a college education shall be limited to the price of a four-year public in-state institution, unless the parties agree otherwise. It should be noted, too, that few students finish a college degree in four years anymore.

TAKEAWAYS

Child support encompasses many issues. Put your children's needs ahead of any anger or problems that you have with your spouse. Do what is best for your family — and that means not fighting over every dime of child support.

Notes

Notes

CHAPTER 27

MANAGING CONFLICTS

MANAGING CONFLICT Q&A

The following responses should be considered as food for thought — ideas and suggestions to be considered. Every circumstance is different, and some responses may not apply to your particular circumstances. You need to think all situations through on your own and do what you think is best.

PARENTAL UNRELIABILITY

When my ex-partner fails to show up or upsets my child in some other important way, how do I address my child's disappointment and hurt?

Remember that although you would like to protect your child from all upset, you are responsible for your behavior, but not for that of your ex-partner. Make sure that you are reliable to your child. Your role is more of helping to observe, realize, and manage some of the problematic results of the other parent's behavior.

Most important is to take time to deal with your child. Do not focus on agreeing or disagreeing, but, rather, focus on listening. Focus on the child's experience, and provide support. Avoid reinforcing negative statements about the shortcomings of the other parent, as tempting as that may be. The focus should be on encouraging resilience in your child and not encouraging criticism of the other parent. Everyone's circumstances are different. In this described circumstance, try to encourage the child to have a positive time with you in the present. Also, possible behaviors can include notifying your attorney, especially if the failure to show up, for example, is a repeat problem.

ENVIRONMENTAL INCONSISTENCY

What do I do when ground rules and discipline are very different in my ex-partner's household? How do I address this with my child?

Keep in mind that you are responsible for your household and the other parent is responsible for his/hers. Consistency is most important in your household, but you cannot control for consistency between the two households. The best you can do is to try to manage the differences.

You can talk with your ex-partner about your observation that your child is having challenges in adjusting to two very different approaches. You can try to work with him/her to make the ground rules and discipline more similar, if (s)he is amenable to talk in a non-defensive and non-judgmental way. It is, of course, possible that such differences were part of the disharmony when you were together.

As for your child, acknowledge to him/her that there may be differences between the two households. Do not paint your approach as good and the other parent's as bad. That does not help the child, but would polarize the situation and magnify the differences. When your household is predictable, it will be best for your child and (s)he will adjust over time.

PARALLEL MISTREATMENT

Sometimes I observe that my ex-partner is treating my child in a manner that is very similar to how I was treated by him/her. I feel very sympathetic and want to tell my child that I know how that feels. How do I manage that situation?

Be understanding, but keep your experience separate from that of the child. First of all, can you be sure that the ex really is treating your child as you were treated? Or is it possible that to some extent you might be framing things that way more than what might actually be accurate? Most importantly, do not make statements to your child that reflect that connection. It will not help the child to deal with whatever issues are going on. Your experience, even if similar, is not likely to be experienced by your child in the same way. You do not want to create an unhealthy alliance with your child involving adult relationship issues.

Instead, deal directly with what your child is experiencing. Without describing it as such, you can make suggestions to the child that seemed to work for you in dealing with the same behavior. Again, do not state that there is any parallel and keep the focus on the child's experience, not on what you experienced.

INAPPROPRIATE PARENTAL BEHAVIOR

My ex-partner says very negative things and lies about me to our child. How do I respond to this?

It is just about always wise to stick with the truth, but the tricky part is to avoid putting your child in the middle. When a parent talks about what the ex-partner is doing, that parent puts an undue burden on the child to agree with them and see things from that perspective. The child needs to see things from a child's perspective.

Put yourself in your child's place, not your child as a stand-in for you. Talk to your child about how (s)he felt at the time. Talk to your child about your own relationship with them, emphasizing positive aspects. It is important that you convey to your child a sense of your strength. If you do this, they may also feel stronger if that situation of negativity recurs.

CHILD EMOTIONAL DISRUPTION

When my child returns from parenting time, (s)he is agitated, moody, and oppositional. I wonder if something is going on in the other household that is causing this problem. How do I handle this situation?

Typically there is a transition period when children return from the other parent. Leaving the other parent and coming to you, your child is adjusting to a new environment, one with different people, different physical circumstances, perhaps different rules — certainly different personalities. This is particularly observed if the time has been longer, such as an overnight or a weekend.

Children may react in different ways, and a negative reaction does not necessarily mean things are bad there or bad with you. The child is adjusting. Different children handle such adjustment differently, depending on their own personalities and ages, and depending on their experience of the relationship between their parents. If possible, parents should agree to try to make the exchange neutral and non-stressful for their child. The focus should be on the experience of the child, not on the attitudes and feelings of the parents.

MAKE THE MOST OF TIME TOGETHER

When my child stays at my house, he/she is often withdrawn and uncommunicative. When I ask how school is going, the answer is just, "Fine." What can I do to get more out of our time together?

Focus on spending sufficient time with your child. Time does not have to be goal-directed, purposive, or structured. Open-ended time also can be desirable. Try to ask specific questions — not just those that can be answered yes or no. Talk about what has been on your mind, such as interesting experiences you have had or things that you have thought about. As you talk, draw comparisons and ask for observations and opinions by him/her of his/her experiences. Ask your child what he/she would like to do. Talk of the past, present, and future, with a focus on the positive.

At some point, state that you want the child to enjoy the time with you. Ask if there is anything you can do to make that improve. Ask if there is anything the child could do differently to make for a better time.

Ask children if they feel uncomfortable about anything. Make clear to them that they do not have to solve any problems or help any situation. Consider if they might feel they are "in the middle" between their parents. You can ask them if they feel that way. If they do feel that way, talk to them about what you yourself can do to reduce that feeling.

MAINTAINING BOUNDARIES

My ex-partner sends me very angry, inappropriate, and negative texts and voicemails. Do I share these with my child to show him/her what I am going through with the other parent?

Do not share inappropriate and negative texts and voicemails. We suggest not sharing any communications intended for adults. Part of being a positive parent is trying to shelter your child from adult concerns and problems. Children are not equipped to deal with adult problems, but adults are. Often children come to feel it is their job to help. It is not their job. It is their job to be a child. If a child is not sheltered from these issues, the child then often tries to get involved. A child cannot solve or even help adults with their problems, especially if the problems involve the other parent. Unfortunately, when they are unsuccessful at mediating or whatever they are doing, they may feel bad at their lack of success. Children need to focus on being children. Their development is important and should not be mixed with adult concerns.

PHYSICAL CONDITION OF CHILDREN

When my child comes home from visitation with their other parent, (s)he is often tired from staying up too late and is poorly groomed, with uncombed hair and rumpled clothing. My child sometimes reports eating junk food and box cereal for dinner rather than warm, nutritious food. What should I do?

You can talk to the child's physician and have the professional assess how the child is doing health-wise. If the child is staying up too late and has been eating junk food, if the other parent has a relationship with the doctor, they could speak with the doctor. Health, and also safety, jointly are priority number one.

It may be undesirable for the child to stay up too late, and there may be consequences such as reduced school performance if the child attends school. Talk to your child's teacher about the child's school functioning and condition when they come to school. If the other parent has a relationship with the teacher, that information can be conveyed during teacher conferences, for example.

All this said, we think it is important to prioritize. Among multiple problems, you may need to choose those that are most important to address for the best interests of your child. It is possible that in your particular circumstances, rumpled clothing and uncombed hair are not a high enough priority to focus on. Consider that if your child is safe and comfortable in the other parent's home, perhaps you can learn to ignore or deprioritize some of this.

(For more, see the supplemental questions in Chapter 30.)

Notes

Notes

_____

_____

_____

_____

_____

_____

_____

_____

_____

_____

_____

_____

_____

_____

_____

_____

_____

_____

_____

_____

_____

_____

_____

_____

_____

_____

_____

_____

_____

CHAPTER 28

MODIFICATION OF CHILD CUSTODY

Once custody and parenting time are set, how difficult is it to modify or change?

The laws vary from state to state. The requirements for a change or modification of the custody of your child also can vary from judge to judge. Some judges are more lenient about modifying custody or parenting time based on changes in circumstances. Others take the attitude that unless there is a significant reason, no change will be granted. This is an area of the law that is very fact specific. Judges look at these situations through the prism of their background and worldview.

There are several aspects of the circumstances that must be considered in determining if there is a basis for modifying custody or parenting time.

It is often difficult to modify custody and parenting time if the schedule is fairly equally divided between the parents. Reasons for a change to be considered could include that the arrangement is not working. For example, one parent may have developed some serious problems, and therefore a change is necessary.

Examples could include an alcohol or drug-related problem or parental involvement with the criminal justice system. There could also be a problem where a child has special needs and one parent can devote more time to deal with the needs of the child.

In Michigan, there is a high threshold to modify custody. However, there is a lower threshold for changing a parenting time schedule, as long as it is not a disguised attempt to change custody.

We have a trend for shared custody arrangements that can be equal or close to equal. Many judges start from the position that custody and parenting time should be a 50-50 schedule or something close to it.

WHEN MODIFICATION MAY BE NEEDED

Let's start from one end of the spectrum where one parent has primary physical custody and the other parent has a limited schedule of alternate weekends from Friday overnight until Sunday evening along with alternate holidays. What might it take to modify that schedule?

If the schedule involves a very young child, an argument can be made that as the child gets older, it is important that he or she have frequent contact with both parents and therefore there should be an increase in parenting time.

For example, there could be an increase in weekend time — possibly the addition of a Sunday overnight so that weekends extend to Monday morning, with the parent who now would have the child on Sunday overnight being responsible for taking the child to school on Monday morning.

Another option could be to add a midweek overnight during the off-week, with the result being that the schedule for the non-custodial parent would be increased from two overnights of 14 to four or five overnights (depending on the weekend) in 14 nights. Other variables may be important to consider, including the age of the child and the effect on the child of the parenting time changes under consideration.

Arguments could be made that what makes sense for a young child may no longer work for a child in elementary school. As children grow, there can be arguments to modify the schedule, especially if an older child wants to spend more time with a parent. This can be especially important as a child becomes a teen. There is the old saying that a teenager is like a 900-pound gorilla — where he or she sits, he or she stays.

It also needs to be considered that children can be manipulative in a divorce or post-divorce situation, and may play one parent against the other. They will say that Dad will allow this or Mom is agreeing to that. One parent may be more of a disciplinarian. One may have looser restrictions on bedtime. The examples are endless. Neither parent would want to be caught in a "bidding war" where the parent with the more appealing car or the offer of a new cell phone or higher allowance is the one who should spend more time with the child.

Other reasons for modifying the schedule can include the fact that a parent has moved in closer proximity to the child. If a parent who had lived 20 miles away is now less than a mile away, this can make it easier for a flow back and forth between two houses.

A change of jobs or work schedules could also be a basis for modifying the schedule. If a parent now has a job with flex time or has the ability to work several days a week from home, this can be relevant. Changing from a job with a heavy travel component to one with little or no travel can also be significant.

School-related issues also are a potential basis for changing a schedule, especially if one parent can be better at helping with schooling and homework. In many situations, one parent has been more involved with school projects, homework, and other daily routines than the other. If grades are being affected or there is a need for special assistance, this can become a factor.

Health issues — either of a parent or a child — can be reasons for modifying a parenting time schedule. If a child is allergic to pets and one parent has a pet, this can become a hindrance. If one parent is more available for a child with serious or chronic health problems, the courts can look at this as well.

Sometimes if a parent or child has mental health or emotional problems, modifying a parenting time schedule may be called for. Examples are where one parent is overtreating a child medically or where there are issues of a parent failing to deal with a serious illness on the part of a child.

As mentioned earlier, criminal behavior of a parent can be a reason for a modification or major adjustment in both parenting time and custody. Examples include when one parent has been arrested for a crime of violence. A parent being arrested for alcohol or drug abuse can be a factor as well.

Domestic violence can also be a basis for modifying a parenting time or custodial arrangement. This is especially true if the child has been a victim or has witnessed the violence.

Parental alienation can be another strong reason for a modification of parenting time or custody and can also be a basis for some significant therapeutic intervention. (*Please see Chapter 11 for more on this topic.*)

In some situations, two siblings may experience significant conflict and perhaps there should be a modification of the schedule so that each parent can have time with each child part of the time, separate from the other sibling.

The safety of the home environment can be relevant if there is an unsafe or hazardous condition. This can be a house where one parent is a heavy smoker and a child has asthma. Black mold can be an issue if it is significant enough, as can a situation where a child is forced to live in a basement that is poorly heated or ventilated.

If one parent is now involved with someone else and the children are being exposed to someone who may be unsavory or can be a threat, this can be a strong basis for changing the custodial or parenting time arrangements.

Problematic use of social media and child exposure to pornography or other inappropriate internet content can be a reason for a modification to be considered as well.

Changes of circumstance in which severe economic problems may have developed and one parent can no longer afford to properly take care of a child can be another reason for adjusting a parenting time arrangement. A parent losing his or her job or being forced to work substantial overtime can be factors.

NEXT STEPS

Consider your current situation and whether it is working in the best interests of your child or children — not what you want, but what is best for them. If you really believe that a change is necessary, then you should write down the reasons and rationale.

If you are serious about changing a custody or parenting time arrangement, consider talking to an attorney. You can receive a considered opinion to see if a change is warranted, and whether or not it will meet the requirements of the courts and laws where you and the children reside.

Don't threaten the other parent and don't quickly or easily go to court. You may lose and will also likely be remembered by your judge. Judges remember those who are repetitively in court, often with insufficient basis.

A final note: We have discussed the importance of keeping a journal and a calendar in Chapter 18, and that is especially important here. If a parent is not following the written schedule that is set forth in a divorce judgment or custody order, adjusting it to mirror the reality that you and the other parent have followed for a year or more can be a reason for modification. And documenting the reality in writing can be very helpful in making that case.

TAKEAWAYS

It is important to remember that one size does not fit all indefinitely. There are numerous reasons for modifying an existing custody and parenting time schedule. The best approach is to have both parents sit down and acknowledge that what they have been doing has not been working, and then come up with a solution to improve the arrangements for their children.

Notes

Notes

CHAPTER 29

RECAP & FINAL THOUGHTS

We have tried to provide information and advice from legal and psychological perspectives to help you understand and navigate the legal system. Our framework has emphasized the best interests of your children. This may not always be consistent with your initial assumptions.

We have covered issues faced by divorcing parents as well as parents who have never wed, or who may have conceived a child as the result of an extremely short relationship.

We have also explored circumstances involving same-sex couples with children. This area is changing rapidly. Here the laws differ from state to state, and it is imperative that you consult with an attorney for the most up-to-date legal information and advice.

Technology, including the internet and social media, permeates our world and can significantly affect custody and parenting time disputes. We have also explored the issues that couples confront when dealing with substance abuse issues relating to alcohol and drugs.

Other major topics we have addressed include parental alienation and domestic violence. All are factors that can affect the best interests of your child or children.

Many cases call for involvement from experts including guardians and mental health professionals such as psychologists, psychiatrists, and social workers. In some high-conflict custody disputes, a psychological evaluation will be required.

We have described techniques to help you through the legal process, including journal writing, calendars, and others.

We have discussed the initial consultation with your attorney and with a mental health professional as well as how to prepare for trial — and most of all, how to stay out of court.

We have included real-life experiences including the use of mediators and common sense so that you have as much knowledge as possible to stay out of court and keep control of your life and those of your children. This is advice that judges give time and again. The last thing that a judge wants to be is Solomon, forced to split the baby in two. The best decisions are always the ones that you make in an adult manner on behalf of your children.

Chapters also explored issues involving moves out of state and international custody disputes.

We also explored grandparent visitation issues and the impact of blended families and new relationships on your children.

Our advice is general in nature and does not replace your need for legal representation or consultation with a mental health professional. Our goal is to make you a more informed client so that you can more effectively work with your attorney and/or psychotherapist.

Remember that your attorney or psychotherapist continues on to their next case while you and your children live with what happens in your custody or parenting time dispute. The events that happen while you go through a custody case will shape your lives and those of your children. The more acrimony there is, the more pain there will be for your children. Never forget that they are the innocent victims of your dispute. You are the adults, and your children rely upon you for their upbringing and guidance. You are their role models.

The goal is for your children to feel free to love each parent and to have the most opportunities and the best possible chance for a healthy life, even though you and your spouse or significant other are no longer living together.

We know that we cannot address every issue that you may face regarding your children and their upbringing, but our goal has been to open the door and let you see as many options as possible for you to explore as you move through the difficult transition to raising your children separately. Even in these new circumstances, you still must communicate with your former partner on ways to give your children as much support as possible with the least conflict so that they can grow up to be healthy, happy, and productive adults.

We hope that we have met our goals and that this book can be a useful tool for you as you move forward.

—Henry S. Gornbein, Esq., and Jack P. Haynes, Ph.D.

CHAPTER 30

FOOD FOR THOUGHT Q&A

SUPPLEMENTAL QUESTIONS AND SUGGESTIONS

The responses to the following questions are ideas and suggestions to consider — food for thought — for commonly occurring situations. There may be other factors to consider in your specific situation. It often may be beneficial to consult with a professional familiar with your own circumstances.

Q. What should a parent do if a child reports the other parent may be under the influence of a substance, or if that parent comes to pick up the child and appears to be under the influence of a substance?

A. Reports or observations of a parent under the influence of a substance while caring for a child should always be considered seriously and evaluated regarding safety concerns. If your child reports that their other parent is "acting different" or is using substances during parenting time, you can contact your attorney to develop a plan for assessment of the situation. Remember that a child, depending on age, can misperceive adult circumstances. Other adults must intervene and make decisions in the child's best interests.

Always consider that the safety of your child is paramount. Try to set aside emotions and judgment for the moment. It is best for the child if all communications about a substance issue are addressed in a calm, careful manner so that the child does not have to absorb any additional emotional strife from either parent.

If you yourself observe the other parent to be under the influence of drugs or alcohol when picking up your child, more immediate action may be required. If you feel able to speak directly to the other parent, you might say something like, "You don't seem to be yourself right now. I'm wondering if you have been drinking. I'm not comfortable in letting you drive with our child and so I can't release him/her to you at this time."

Additionally, or as an alternative, you can call the police and explain your concerns for your child's safety. Police are often experienced in custody and parenting time issues. The police are also equipped to make an immediate assessment regarding sobriety and safety. If they conclude safety has been compromised or is about to be, the police can intervene so the immediate situation can be resolved calmly and safely.

Q. My child often refuses to go on parenting time. What do I say? What do I do?

A. If children are strongly resistant to spending time with the other parent, it is time to have a talk with them. Find a quiet spot where there will be no interruptions. Establish good eye contact and ask open-ended questions that allow your child to answer in full.

Examples of open-ended questions could be:
• Tell me why you don't want to go to Mom's/Dad's house.

- Tell me more. I want to make sure I understand. Is this what you are saying? (Repeat what the child said.)
- What would make it better?
- Try to reflect your child's feelings. Ask if you have it right.

If adjustments can be made, you can try to problem solve with the child. If the child is still resistant, explain to the child that this is the co-parenting plan that Mom and Dad agreed was best. The conversation itself is helpful. You don't have to solve the problem. You want the child to feel understood and to see you as a resource. The conversation is the point, and you can engage in potential problem-solving.

Your attorney needs to be informed of the general issues of your child's reluctance to go. This also is true if the child works with a counselor or psychotherapist, or if a GAL is involved. Any substantive issues can be addressed with a neutral party.

Q. My child wants to spend more time at my ex-partner's house. This hurts my feelings and disappoints me. How do I respond to this?

A. It is very understandable that your feelings would be hurt and you might feel a bit rejected. But keep in mind good parenting is not a popularity contest. Review your parenting goals and make sure your household is consistent with these goals. Talk with a friend who is a parent or talk with a professional to get emotional support and feedback regarding your concerns.

You can also talk with your child to find out what makes the other household so appealing. Listen carefully and patiently while imagining your child's experience. There might be some things you can resolve, but maybe not. There may be some things you might approve of, or maybe not. But you can give assurance to your child that you love them and always will strive to do what is best for them.

Q. Just before I take my young child back to my ex-partner's household, he starts to cry and say he does not want to leave, and would rather stay with me. How do I manage this situation?

A. It is important to remember that the changes sometimes involved with co-parenting are significant and stressful to a child. This can be true even when both households are safe and nurturing. There often are many changes that can be challenging, such as change of locale or different household rules and expectations.

Younger children can become irritable, clingy — even tearful — just prior to co-parenting time exchanges. Adolescents, who are often more interested in spending time with their peers, may find changes disruptive and annoying. It is important not to put too much significance on the normal limits resistance that children often exhibit. It does not necessarily signify that one parent is better or worse than another. It is often change itself that children seek to avoid since uncertainty and adjustments are involved.

Be comforting and reassuring to your child. Remind him that you will be there when he returns. Encourage the child to enjoy time and experiences with the other parent.

Q. When I come to pick up my child for prearranged co-parenting time, there is often conflict or confrontation with my ex-partner. What do I do?

A. Most importantly, try to shield your child from the conflict. She will not benefit from direct experience of parental conflict, and more likely the observation of such conflict will be disruptive to her in some ways. Try not to have your child be an observer of the strife.

For example, try to take her out of the situation — have her go in the house and suggest an activity in which she can engage there. Try to avoid demonstration and overt expression of anger, even if the ex-partner is demonstrating that. Keep in mind your ex-partner may intentionally be provocative. That provocation will not be for your benefit. Nothing is likely to be resolved under emotionally aroused conditions. Defusing is desirable, but it is not always possible to agree in the moment. You are not responsible for the other person, but you are responsible for yourself and your own actions as they affect your child.

If the conflict begins to escalate in a way about which you have concern or the situation seems to becoming unsafe, you can consider calling the police. Keep in mind, most often the presence of the police should only be to assure safety, not as a tool to "up the ante" and to cause problems for the ex-partner.

Q. What do I do if during parenting time, my young child starts to cry for the other parent?

A. Young children in particular are apt to miss a parent with whom they are closely attached, especially in times of heightened need or in momentary crisis. For example, a child might want the other parent during an illness or while experiencing fear. It is often helpful to reach out with affection and reassurance. Do not take the reaction as a personal rejection, but rather give voice to your child's feelings. For example, you could say something like, "I know you miss your mom/dad, but I am here with you and I will help you feel better."

Moving on to a fun activity (a bowl of ice cream, a card game — whatever simple option pleases) helps the child to cope and reestablish a sense of safety and comfort. This might actually be an opportunity to reinforce your own bond with your child.

Q. What if my child calls me during the parenting time of the other parent and says that they do not want to be there, they are bored, or are being treated unfairly. How do I respond?

A. It is quite common for a child to prefer, at times, one household over another. The reasons can vary (better electronics; fewer rules and responsibilities; more neighborhood friends; reasons you do not know, etc.). Even when estranged parents strive for consistency (a rare circumstance) households differ and each parent creates a unique experience for a child.

If you get a complaining call while your child is visiting the other parent, it can help if you listen patiently without saying much. Let your child know you understand their feelings. Unless there is an issue with safety, tell your child that you both, as their parents, have agreed on the custody schedule and you will be seeing each other soon. The focus is allowing the child to be heard, even while the situation will not be changed. You do not necessarily need to provide answers; this is the best response for now.

Depending on the age of your child, the nature of the complaint, and the relationship of the child with the other parent, it may be useful to see if it is feasible for the child to talk with the other parent about the problem. Depending on circumstances, it also may be feasible for you to talk to the other parent. If the child has a counselor or psychotherapist, it may be important for that person to know of the issue.

Try to encourage problem-solving and resiliency in your child. Of course, this approach needs to be adapted to your child's age, developmental level, and relationship with you and the other parent.

Q. What can parents do to mitigate the risks to their children in these situations?
A. As in any parental situation, you cannot make all things right for your children. But you can do your best. And if your children are truly your priority, act that way — it's not a concept.

Time. Most important, job one, numero uno: spend time with your children. Prioritize time each day — time that is open-ended and unstructured — to just sit and talk. Observe. See what is important to them. Ask how they are doing and listen to their answers. Get down on their level. Engage in their world.

Consistency. This is essential. Children learn by example, even if they might not like what they are experiencing from you at the time. In part, children come to understand how the world works through their experience of parental consistency, which is how they learn limits. They learn what is allowed and what isn't. You are their number one role model through the years of intense learning.

Discuss. Talk to your children about your observations, reasoning, and conclusions. Tell them that it is your best decision, and that they will have to go with it for now. You (and your partner) are the parents, and they are the child. Do your best. Tell them that is your best, and that they will have to go with the best for now, even if it's not ideal: "I'm going to use my best judgment because you are so important to me."

Be Involved. We can tell you that throughout our careers we have heard over and over from current parents that they wish one or both of their parents had been more involved with them. While the past cannot be changed, the present and future can be. What does this mean? Know where your children are at all times. Know your children's friends and the parents of those friends. Go to your children's sporting activities, including practices, as much as you can. Keep in touch with their teachers.

Coordinate. One of the hallmarks of a deteriorating relationship is that decisions between the partners are often not in sync. This almost inevitably affects the children of such a relationship. We encourage our clients to separate the partner estrangement from being good parents and work together as much as possible. Children benefit from parents, though separate, who can at least be united when it comes to the child's well-being.

Involve Others. It can be important for your children, if possible, to have frequent access to the members on both sides of their extended family. Despite their imperfections, human frailties, and oddities, extended family can be an important support system for your children. Besides having interesting, enjoyable, and new experiences, your children can learn that others besides their parents also care about them.

Notes

APPENDIX

1

SAMPLE QUESTIONS FOR TRIAL

APPENDIX I

Sample Questions for Trial

As mentioned earlier in this book, Michigan judges must take into consideration 12 children's Best Interests Factors in every child custody or parenting time case. These suggested questions are just meant to scratch the surface, and provide food for thought.

1. **The love, affection, and other emotional ties existing between the parties involved and the child:**
   (1) Who gets your child breakfast, lunch, and dinner?
   (2) What are your child's favorite foods?
   (3) Favorite TV programs and stories?
   (4) Favorite games and toys?
   (5) What are your child's interests and hobbies?
   (6) How would you describe the relationship of your child with the other parent? How would you describe your relationship with your child?
   (7) How has your child been reacting to your separation?
   (8) What would you do in response to the child's reactions?
   (9) How would you view the bond and ties of your child with the other parent? Are they equal?
   (10) If you feel that you have a closer relationship with your child than the other parent, what are the reasons?
   (11) How does your child know that you love him or her?
   (12) How do you show love to your child?
   (13) What do you believe that your children would say if asked about your relationship with them?
   (14) Who does your child turn to if there is a problem?
   (15) Who does your child turn to when sick or hurt?
   (16) Who does your child turn to for sharing events or the daily activities?

2. **The capacity and disposition of the parties involved to give the child love, affection, and guidance and continuation of any educating and raising of the children in their religion or creed, if any.**
   (1) Who feeds your child? What kind of food do you feed your child?
   (2) Who gives baths?
   (3) Who changes diapers?
   (4) Who stays home from work if a child is sick?
   (5) What is the work schedule of the other parent versus yours?
   (6) Who takes care of school arrangements and enrollment?
   (7) How is religious education handled?

(8) What about parent-teacher conferences?

(9) What about other school activities?

(10) How are decisions made with the other parent?

(11) Who puts your child to bed?

(12) Who gets your child up in the morning?

(13) Who gets your child to school in the morning?

(14) Who reads bedtime stories or handles other nightly activities?

(15) How do you teach your child manners?

(16) How does the other parent teach the child manners?

(17) How is discipline handled by you?

(18) How is discipline handled by the other parent?

(19) Do you ever disagree over discipline?

(20) What is a typical day in the life of your child?

(21) What is your religious practice and that of the other parent?

(22) How do you each handle your child's fears or insecurities?

(23) What are your positive and negative parenting skills? The other parent's?

(24) How do you show your child love and affection?

(25) What kind of activities do you do with your child?

(26) If there are issues involving anger, how are they dealt with?

(27) What is your involvement with your child's schooling and extracurricular activities? What about the other parent?

(28) Are there rules in the home?

(29) How is homework handled?

(30) Is there anything else that you can add on this theme?

3. **The capacity and disposition of the parents involved to provide the child with food, clothing, medical care, or other remedial care recognized and permitted under the laws of this state in place of medical care, and other material needs.**

(1) Who purchases your child's clothing, toys, and any other items?

(2) Who takes care of medical and dental appointments?

(3) Who takes care of a therapist appointment, if any?

(4) Who takes care of babysitters and child care?

(5) If there are any special medical or educational needs, how are these handled?

(6) Who is better able to deal with any special needs? What are the special needs, if any?

(7) Who is better in a crisis and why?

(8) How is money handled?

(9) What is your income?

(10) What is the income of the other parent?

(11) How do you feel the other parent handles finances and money management?

(12) If you are working, what arrangements will be made regarding day care and other care for your child when he or she is not in school?

4. **The length of time the child has lived in a stable, satisfactory environment, and the desirability of maintaining continuity.**
   (1) Describe the home where your children currently reside.
   (2) Describe the proposed custodial home.
   (3) How will any move likely affect your child?
   (4) How are bedrooms and sleeping handled now?
   (5) How will they be handled in the proposed home?
   (6) What adjustments do you see regarding any move?
   (7) Where are your child's friends and relatives?
   (8) Are there any safety issues regarding the proposed custodial home or neighborhood?
   (9) How will the move affect school, extracurricular activities, and friends?
   (10) Is there anything that you can add for the court?

5. **The permanence, as a family unit, of the existing or proposed custodial home or homes.**
   (1) What is the child's relationship to any other siblings?
   (2) What is the child's relationship with his or her parents?
   (3) What changes will there be with the proposed new home?
   (4) How will the move affect relationships with family members? Friends? Schoolmates?
   (5) Are there plans for a remarriage?
   (6) Will you be continuing a relationship with a significant other?
   (7) Are there any plans to live together with a significant other?
   (8) How is the relationship of a significant other with your child?
   (9) Is there anything else that you can add that would be of assistance to the court?

6. **The moral fitness of the parents involved.**
   (1) Is there any involvement with alcohol or drugs by either parent? What about stepparents?
   (2) What about marijuana?
   (3) Are there any issues regarding prescription drugs?
   (4) Has there been any treatment in the past?
   (5) Is there any treatment at the present time?
   (6) Are there any romantic liaisons by either parent?
   (7) Have the children been involved with any friends or significant others of either parent?
   (8) Is foul language used in front of the child by either parent? If so, what impact has this had on the child?
   (9) Has there been any inappropriate activity on the internet or on social media that may have been seen by your child? Text messages? Emails?

(10) What are your moral strengths and weaknesses? What about those of the other parent?

(11) Have there been any allegations of physical or sexual abuse of the child or any other children by you or the other parent? What about by a stepparent or significant other?

(12) Are there any issues regarding either parent driving under the influence of alcohol or drugs?

(13) Has your child ever been exposed to inappropriate behavior? Inappropriate movies or internet sites?

(14) Have there been any issues regarding criminal involvement?

(15) Are there any issues regarding anger management by you or the other parent?

(16) Is there any issue regarding alienation with you or the other parent?

(17) Have you tried to undermine the other parent? What about vice versa?

(18) Is there anything else that you can add regarding this factor?

7. The mental and physical health of the parties involved.

(1) How is your physical health? The other parent's?

(2) How about mental health for both parents?

(3) Are there any issues regarding hospitalizations or psychotherapy on your part or that of the other parent?

(4) Are there any physical or mental health issues that could affect custody and/or parenting time?

(5) Is there anything else that you can add to assist the court?

8. The home, school, and community record of the child.

(1) Where does your child attend school?

(2) What is your child's attendance record?

(3) What about grades?

(4) Have there been disciplinary issues regarding your child in school?

(5) How does your child view school?

(6) What extracurricular activities is your child involved in?

(7) What is your involvement in these activities? The other parent's?

(8) What are your child's chores at home?

(9) How involved have you been regarding homework? Regarding chores at home? And what about the other parent?

(10) Has there been any involvement with any juvenile courts or other agencies regarding your family or child?

(11) How is your child's relationship with friends?

(12) What about involvement with any community activities?

9. The reasonable preference of the child, if the court deems the child to be of sufficient age to express a preference. (This is a tricky issue because in many cases, each parent believes that he or she is the preferred parent. Often each parent is wrong. This issue is explored in detail in Chapter 24, which deals with the preference of a child from a judge's perspective.)
    (1) How do you think your child will react to a change of custody?
    (2) Do you think that your child has a preference? If so, why?
    (3) Why are you seeking custody?

10. The willingness and ability of each parent to facilitate and encourage a close and continuing parent-child relationship. (This is a critical factor, especially where issues of parental alienation or abuse come into play. It also goes to issues regarding the ability of two parents to communicate and co-parent. Judges view this factor as important.)
    (1) What is your proposed parenting time schedule?
    (2) Do you talk about the other parent in front of the child? If so, what do you say?
    (3) Do you ever denigrate or speak ill of the other parent in front of the child? Does the other parent ever do this about you?
    (4) How do you and the other parent get along?
    (5) What is the best thing that you can say about the other parent? About yourself?
    (6) What is the worst thing that you can say about the other parent? What is the worst thing the other parent could say about you?

11. Domestic violence, regardless of whether the violence was directed against or witnessed by the child. Here, issues of parental alienation, as well as control, can come into play as well. This is a very important area of the child custody act.
    (1) Have there been any instances of verbal abuse? Emotional abuse?
    (2) In cases where there is physical or emotional abuse, it is important to carefully detail the situation with names, dates, who, what, where, and when.

12. Any other factors considered by the court to be relevant to a particular child custody dispute.
    This is a catch-all that can be used for almost anything that has not already been covered. It is a factor for the judge to give a reason for a decision that may have not been covered under any of the other best interests factors.

Notes

ABOUT THE AUTHORS

Attorney Henry S. Gornbein, Esq., is a leading expert in family law. Practicing in Michigan for more than 40 years, he is an attorney with the Cronin Law Firm in Bloomfield Hills, Michigan.

Gornbein is a former Chairperson of the Family Law Section of the State Bar of Michigan. He is also a past President of the Michigan Chapter of the American Academy of Matrimonial Lawyers.

Gornbein has written extensively on divorce-related topics and is the author of *Divorce Demystified*, which focuses on the steps that couples go through during divorce. He also produces regular podcasts for *divorcesourceradio.com* and has hosted and produced his own Philo Award-winning cable TV show, *Practical Law*. In addition, Gornbein has been speaking for a series of webinars discussing the impact of social media on divorce, along with issues including wiretapping, computer hacking, spycams, and others that can arise during divorce and have criminal law violation implications.

A frequent public speaker for local and national meetings, he has been a featured lecturer at the National Convention of the American Academy of Matrimonial Lawyers.

Henry is the creator and host of the video series "Gracefully Greying," which can be found at *www.gracefullygreying.com*.

Jack P. Haynes, Ph.D., is a distinguished and highly respected psychologist with more than 40 years of forensic psychological experience. Having performed thousands of evaluations in a variety of domestic and non-domestic cases, Dr. Haynes has conducted more than 700 court-ordered psychological evaluations related specifically to child custody and parenting time. He is a seasoned expert witness and also has been appointed as Parenting Coordinator in numerous high-conflict circumstances.

In the early years of his career, Dr. Haynes was director of research, training, and clinical services for a large metropolitan juvenile court system. He went on to serve as President of the Michigan Psychological Association, President of the Michigan Society of Forensic Psychology, and Chair of the Michigan Psychology Licensing Board. Most recently, he has been Chair of the Ethics Committee of the American Psychological Association in Washington, D.C. Dr. Haynes consults with attorneys on domestic relations and other matters, and he often has presented to judicial, legal, and psychological groups.